The Heart of t

M000197795

Individuation as an Ethical Process

Christina Becker

2nd Edition

Chiron Publications
Asheville, North Carolina

ISBN   978-1-63051-071-8   paperback
ISBN   978-1-63051-072-5   hard cover

Library of Congress Cataloging-in-Publication Data
Becker, Christina, 1958–
The heart of the matter : individuation as an ethical process /
Christina Becker.
_____ p. cm.
Includes bibliographical references and index.
ISBN   978-1-63051-071-8   paperback
ISBN   978-1-63051-072-5   hard cover
1. Individuation (Psychology) 2. Psychoanalysis—Moral and ethical aspects. 3. Psychoanalysts—Attitudes. 4.
Psychoanalysts—Psychology. 5. Jungian psychology. I. Title.
RC506.B354 2004
155.2'5—dc22

_____

2004006025

Cover concept, illustration and design by Aries Cheung (Toronto, Canada)
Typesetting and print production by Michael Caplan (Toronto, Canada)

Acknowledgements

I would like to thank my Thesis Committee at the C.G. Jung Institute in Zürich for their guidance and wisdom throughout the writing process; Ursula Wirtz, Waltraut Koerner, and Andreas Schweizer; and Ruth Ammann, Dorothy Gardner, Sonja Marjasch, Annemarie Moser, and Françoise O'Kane. These fine analysts continually challenged my ethical muscles and forced me to reflect on and refine my beliefs, ideas, and assumptions. I am truly grateful for their input. Special thanks also go to those people involved in the survey of analysts that I utilized in the thesis. The creation and pretesting of the survey questions, and the translation into German, French, Italian, and Spanish for the IAAP webpage was done with the assistance of Members of the AGAP Executive Committee, and with financial support from an anonymous donor.

Thanks also to Jacques Beaumont; John Becker; Lois Becker; Mary Benedetto, Natalia Bubica; Katharina Casanova, Deborah Egger; John Granrose; Shirley Halliday; Esther Keller; Nicoletta Lucatelli; Johanna Ohnesorg; Beaty Popescu; Manisha Roy; Judith Slimmon; Hester McFarland Solomon; Donald Williams; Brenda Weinberg; Murray Stein; and Luigi Zoja.

Thank you to Pat Archer, Shirley Halliday, and Beaty Popescu for their help during the last stages of editing of the original manuscript, and for their friendship, and to Pat for introducing me to the circle process and for reminding me of its power.

I would like to acknowledge Murray Stein, Chiron Publications' first publisher, for his confidence in the original work; Steven Buser and Len Cruz, the new owners of Chiron Publications, for their loving embrace and support of a second edition; and Aries Cheung, for his innovative cover design. I would like to thank Michael Caplan for his fine copy editing skills that made the text much more accessible, and for page layout. I am indebted to Kathryn Dean not only for her first-rate editing of the original manuscript, but also for helping me to recover my cat Artemis who had been living on the street for four weeks in July, 2002.

Finally, I want to thank my parents Gwenne and the late John Becker for their love and support throughout my life, and for making it possible for this book to be published through their active participation in the book's production through Becker Associates.

Contents

Preface to the Second Edition

I began writing *The Heart of the Matter: Individuation as an Ethical Process* as a student at the C.G. Jung Institute (Zurich) in Küsnacht, Switzerland. The material became my thesis that led to my graduation in 2002, and in 2004, it was published in a cooperative effort between Chiron Publications and Becker Associates.

In reviewing the material for this edition, I found that some of it required updating. For example, several important contributions to the literature have been published that shed light on Jung's life that were not previously understood and known. Specifically I am referring to *The Red Book*, edited by Sonu Shamdasani (2009), and Deidre Bair's biography (2004). Information and insights from these books have deepened my understanding of Jung and his relationship to individuation and to ethics.

In the original text, the material in Chapter 5 which discussed "Jung's Ethical Confrontation with the Unconscious" was based almost exclusively on *Memories, Dreams, Reflections*. This was of course written only a couple of years before Jung's death. While important, it was a reflection of something that happened a number of decades before. Combined with Jung's stated reluctance to publish *The Red Book* in the first place, it is highly probable that Jung minimized the extent of this transformative time in life. As we know now, the product of this confrontation is found in *The Red Book* and we are graced with the *prima materia* from that time.

I have added relevant material that reflects current understanding of the field of analytical psychology including contributions to the field by Hester Solomon, Luigi Zoya and others. I removed the survey of analysts that I conducted in 2002 as part of my diploma thesis. The data proved to be out of the date and not reflective of current practice. In the end, I hope that this book is a reflective contribution to this discussion and that it is accessible to therapists and non-therapists as we journey through this minefield called life.

Introduction

To be ethical is work, and it is the essential human task. Human beings cannot look "above" for what is right and wrong, good or evil; we must struggle with these questions and recognize that, while there are no clear answers, it is still crucial to continue probing further and refining our judgments more precisely. This is an endless process of moral reflection.[1]

—Murray Stein

Morality, conscience, and ethics have occupied the minds of theologians, philosophers, scientists, and psychologists for as long as human beings have wondered about the nature of the universe and the nature of being human. Our moral sense, according to Plato, is a divine gift bestowed by Zeus to ensure our survival and greatness. Humans are ethical creatures. Included in our ethical deliberations, we look for the differentiation between being human and being inhuman and seek answers to fundamental questions such as: Is there a god? What is the meaning of life? How do human beings live harmoniously with each other? What behaviour is acceptable and what is not? And what defines a good person? Our reactions to life's situations act as a barometer based on the degree to which we feel guilt, shame, embarrassment, compassion, anger, outrage, gratitude, and/or forgiveness in different situations. This journey appears to be deeply embedded in our psyches.

My own exploration of these issues came from a personal experience that involved a profound ethical conflict and defined my whole training as a Jungian analyst. Several opposites were constellated in this psychological crisis: collective ethical codes and my individual conscience; the principles of Logos and the values of Eros; the desire for a quick and easy collective solution and the need to remain with my own psychological process in analysis. I felt as if I

---

1   Murray Stein, "Introduction" in *Jung on Evil* (Princeton,. NJ: Princeton University Press, 1996), p. 10.

was in a battle between my ego and some "Other," and this "Other" insisted I heed the values of Eros and introversion while the rationality of Logos and of the collective moral/ethical code was absolutely clear about the impropriety of the situation. In analysis, I was forced into my own ethical confrontation with the unconscious as I came to grips with my Shadow and aspects of my personality that I had repressed. There was no black and white solution to the complexity of the dilemma that I faced. This psychological experience constituted a paralysis of sorts, which prevented me from acting according to the dictates of either position. Instead, I vacillated between opposing attitudes and feelings.

I found comfort and understanding in Jung's description of a "conflict of duty." In his foreword to Erich Neumann's *Depth Psychology and a New Ethic*, Jung writes: "The chief causes of neurosis are conflicts of conscience and difficult moral problems that require an answer."[2] He goes on to name these conflicts as conflicts of duty that arise from a clash between the individual and some outside force. A solution cannot be answered by the collective but must come from somewhere within the individual. For Jung, "the treatment of neurosis is not, in the last resort, a technical problem but a moral one."[3]

While Freud thought that moral law was an expression of outward value, Jung believed this law actually came from within as part of the archetypal level of the human psyche. Jung also wrote in the same foreword to Neumann's book:

> If a man is endowed with an ethical sense and is convinced of the sanctity of ethical values, he is on the surest road to a conflict of duty. And although this looks desperately like a moral catastrophe, it alone makes possible a higher differentiation of ethics and a broadening of consciousness. A conflict of duty forces us to examine our conscience and therefore to discover the Shadow. This, in turn, forces us to come to terms with the unconscious.[4]

The seed of Jung's psychological conception of this moral "conflict of duty" arises out of his personal journey. An early experience of God when Jung was twelve years old was the catalyst for this conflict. The vision propelled him to reconcile his personal experience with what he had been told by the church

---

2   C.G. Jung, "Foreword to Neumann: *Depth Psychology and the New Ethic*" in *The Symbolic Life*, Vol. 18 of *The Collected Works* (Princeton, NJ: Princeton University Press, 1949), paragraph 1408.

3   *Ibid.*, paragraph 1412.

4   *Ibid.*, paragraph 1417.

and his father. In *Memories, Dreams, Reflections,* Jung reports that he was compelled to reconcile these two images in his psyche. In 1912, his journey to reconcile the opposites would deepen following his break with Freud. The result of his descent into the unconscious is captured in *The Red Book: Liber Novus.*[5] His work during this period produced many images, fantasies, and other unconscious material that he studied for the rest of his life. Jung wrestled with the conflict between his public position as an academic and psychiatrist and a deeper calling to pursue his scientific experiment in the fascinating unconscious world that he had just discovered. This intense pull was between what he called the "Spirit of the Times" and the "Spirit of the Depths." Finally, the "Spirit of the Depths" would have the greater call, resulting in Jung's decision to relinquish a number of important worldly positions.

In one of his last papers, "A Psychological View of Conscience" (1958), Jung presents a lifetime of experience on his personal solution to this "conflict of duty." As the reflections of a man at the end of his life, the paper offers us this wisdom while confronting us with the complexity of the issues. Jung writes: "If the voice of conscience is the voice of God, this voice must possess an incomparably higher authority than traditional morality."[6] He goes on: "Conscience—no matter on what it is based, commands the individual to obey his inner voice even at the risk of going astray."[7]

For Jung, this inner "Voice of God" was the voice of individuation and the Self. The Self is the centre of the personality, the inner divinity within each individual that guides one's life and destiny. Individuation, according to Jung, is a natural developmental process within every individual that helps them become the person they were meant to be. In other words, it is a process through which an individual becomes more him- or herself—more authentic and distinct from other people and from collective values and norms.

The moral tension that Jung outlines between the individual and the collective is an archetypal and ancient one. A similar debate can be found in ancient China between the *Tao Te Ching* and the more collective Confucian morality. It is in this dialogue that we find the origins of Jung's major contributions to our understanding of the psyche: the principle of opposition. This concept is imaged in the Taoist Tai Chi symbol showing black and white contained in a circle. It reflects the Eastern philosophy that all psychic life consists

---

5   C.G. Jung, *The Red Book: Liber Novus* (New York: W.W. Norton & Co, 2009).

6   C.G. Jung, "A Psychological View of Conscience" in *Civilization in Transition*, Vol. 10 of *The Collected Works* (Princeton, NJ: Princeton University Press , 1958), paragraph 840.

7   *Ibid.*, paragraph 841.

of dualities such as light–dark, masculine–feminine, white–black, Sun–Moon, and right–wrong. Jung recognized this principle as "the ineradicable and indispensable pre-condition of all psychic life,"[8] and said that it "constitutes the phenomenology of the paradoxical self, man's totality."[9] He saw that it was inherent in a psychic system that was naturally self-regulating and self-healing.

It is this conflict within the psyche that Jung felt was the cause of neurosis or psychological distress and the precondition for psychic development and consciousness. It is the clash of two values "that shows the polarity of the psyche."[10] Jung goes on to write that "Conscience brings the ever-present and necessary opposites to conscious perception."[11]

The opposites first appear in an undifferentiated way: they are experienced as irreconcilable, with no immediate solution. It is the tension and the irreconcilability of the situation that results in neurotic symptoms. However, when the collision between two opposing forces becomes so intense, a solution must be found, and the two elements are reconciled in a new, more differentiated way. The solution is a non-rational one, that is, it cannot be fashioned by the rational mind. Jung saw the third or reconciling element coming from a symbol that is acceptable to both opposing forces and that can unite the opposites. He named this element the transcendent function and saw it as the mediator of the individual's conflict of duty. "The resolution of the conflict comes from the appearance of the reconciling motif such as that of the orphan or abandoned child. Rather than opposition, there now appears as a new born configuration, symbolic of the nascent whole, a figure possessing potentials beyond those that the conscious mind has yet been able to conceive."[12]

The symbol expressed by the transcendent function has an important teleological function, that is, it has a psychic purpose: it is the psyche's means of evolution. When the transcendent function can rise above the human condition and carry with it a particularly numinous quality, it is connected to the God-Image or the Self, thus to Jung's notion of conscience as the *Vox Dei*. This connection is the goal of the individuation process, as the Self is the archetype of orientation and meaning. Often it is the symbol of the Child that reflects this new psychic configuration and is the bearer of the Self. The archetype of

---

8   C.G. Jung, *Mysterium Coniunctionis*, Vol. 14 of *The Collected Works* (Princeton NJ: Princeton University Press, 1956), paragraph 206.

9   *Ibid.*, paragraph 4.

10   C.G. Jung. "Conscience," in *The Symbolic Life*, paragraph 844.

11   *Ibid.*, paragraph 844.

12   Andrew Samuels, Bani Shorter, and Fred Plaut, *A Critical Dictionary of Jungian Analysis* (London: Routledge, 1986), p. 103.

the Child also embodies the personality's urge for self-realization. As Jung writes:

> It [The Child] represents the strongest, the most ineluctable urge in every human being, namely the urge to realize itself. It is, as it were, an incarnation of the inability to do otherwise, equipped with all the powers of nature and instinct, whereas the conscious mind is always getting caught up in its supposed ability to do otherwise. The urge and compulsion to self-realization is a law of nature and thus is invincible power.[13]

The symbol of the child is duplicitous because of its link to the past, to remnants of our own childhoods and parts of our personality that are undeveloped, infantile, and repressed, and they are attached to the Shadow because they are deemed to be unacceptable. This means psychologically that the deeper levels of the psyche—of the Self—can only be reached through the undifferentiated, childlike parts of ourselves. It is this aspect of our personality that is also the closest to what Jung called the *inferior function*, i.e. the typological function that is the closest to the unconscious. The child then becomes the Child–Hero who embarks on the perilous journey and overcomes great obstacles toward wholeness. "'Child' means something evolving toward independence. This it cannot do without detaching itself from its origins: abandonment is therefore a necessary condition, not just a concomitant symptom."[14]

Jung's ethical call in the individual voice of implies finding one's own path, separate from the collective. His path of individuation was forged through the painful and emotionally wrought experiences found in *The Red Book*. His journey is likened to a Child–Hero who becomes the Orphan separated from the World–Parents, isolated and expelled from the collective tribe.

The journey through the forest of the unconscious is lonely and introverted. It is necessary to contend with all the negative, destructive, and unpleasant elements contained there, and to challenge ego ideals, perceptions, and conceptions. The strength and ethical response of the ego are needed to meet and accept the Shadow. It is only through this journey that we develop the "right relationship" to our inner world, find our inner morality, and meet the Self—that is, the carrier of the personality's wholeness, integrity, and authenticity. This suggests an implicit connection between wholeness and behaving out of one's integrity, essence, and morality. Individuation is an ethical process.

---

13   C.G. Jung, *The Archetype and the Collective Unconscious*, Vol. 9(i) of *The Collected Works* (Princeton NJ: Princeton University Press:, 1940), paragraph 289.
14   *Ibid.*, paragraph 287.

The identification of this connection is not unique to Jung; it is also found in other writings on ethics and morality, suggesting the universality of the journey. In the context of individuation, as we connect to our wholeness we also connect to our inner morality and values. Jung's own personal work with the unconscious and his writings on the ethical and moral dimensions of individuation illustrate the specific moral challenges that we face when we begin to work with the unconscious. He has also offered us a moral ideal—not, however, as a model of behaviour, but as a model of the necessary attitude and courage that we need if we embark on the same path.

In spite of Jung's strong ethical ideals, he was not above acting out of his own Shadow, and analytical psychology has suffered from this legacy and inherited this flaw. It is widely known that Jung had intimate relationships with at least two of his analysands. Specifically, in the case of Sabina Spielrein, his behaviour around attempts to conceal the nature of their association and to defend himself was far from exemplary, and his career as a young psychiatrist was almost destroyed as a result.

The ethical opposites that Jung outlined in "A Psychological View of Conscience" make up the tension that analytical psychologists face in daily practice today. For many years, a good number of Jungian societies resisted instituting ethical codes governing acceptable behaviour for their members because they felt this would be antithetical to Jung's vision of the individuation process. What was more important, in their view, was the individual's personal code of ethics that would serve to guide analysts through difficult ethical situations. Ethical standards were argued to be ego and rational constructs that would not allow space for the unconscious to speak. Like Freud's collective moral codes, ethical codes have the potential to be a series of "Thou shalt nots" and would legislate the Shadow out of existence.

However, the ethical climate that analytical psychology has faced in the last twenty years has been a particularly challenging one. In many parts of the world, analytical psychology was forced to adapt to collective standards of ethical behaviour as the result of increased government regulation of psychotherapy and psychoanalysis. There is a growing recognition that ethical codes are needed to protect analysands and the public and to preserve the integrity of the profession. Such standards reflect the group norm concerning what is and is not acceptable. Ethical codes help to draw the magic circle—the sacred *temenos*—around analytic work, providing guidelines against which to measure our behaviour. But adaptation to collective rules sets up another conflict of duty between abiding by these rules and following the dictates of the psyche.

Individuation as an ethical process affects analysands as they traverse the unknown waters of the unconscious in the struggle for meaning and wholeness, and it affects analysts as they face the ethical dilemmas of practice and struggle with collective moral norms. As Jung wrote, "ethical values must not be injured on either side if the treatment is to be successful."[15]

Ethical action and reflection lie in the precarious balance between individual conscience and the collective moral code. Like the symbol of the Child, the symbol of the Heart embodies this tension. The Heart is the centre of the psyche, and the centre of the body. It is the seat of the Self—an understanding informed by both Eastern and Western ancient philosophical traditions. The Chinese refer to the "Heart-Mind"—the place of a certain kind of ethical thinking that establishes priorities, assigns values, discerns duties, and recognizes obligations. The Hindus refer to the *Anahata chakra*—the place of compassion, forgiveness, and detachment, where the *purusa* "or the Self" is born.

Psychologically, the Heart performs an integrative psychic function and carries individual morality. The Heart is the place where opposites come together: Logos and Eros; masculine and feminine; thinking and feeling; the rationality of the ego, and the irrationality of the unconscious. It possesses its own knowledge and its own truth. This truth is distinct from the truth of the mind while also containing it. The Heart is the seat of conscience, understanding, forgiveness, grace, and our ethical attitude; it is the place of dialogue. In the Heart, we can be in the ethical attitude of holding both polarities until the new attitude appears.

This book is an inquiry into philosophical and spiritual aspects of individuation's ethical dimensions. Specifically, these aspects are viewed in the context of people actively engaged in their processes and in the practice of analytical psychology. The book is aimed at clients and patients wishing to understand how to live an ethical life when confronted with the amorality of the unconscious and the ethical conflicts of duty that arise. I also hope to serve analysts, therapists, and those in training by providing a framework for thinking and reflecting on these issues.

The work spans many aspects of this complicated topic: Is morality learned or is it innate? How do we live in the world ethically, authentically, and with integrity? What is the distinction between the individual "Voice of God" and collective ethical codes, and how do we live this tension in our lives and in day-to-day practice as analysts? Finally, how do we confront the Shadow in individuals and collectives and bring these elements to consciousness?

---

15 Jung, "Conscience" in *The Symbolic Life*, paragraph 852.

The book is divided into three parts. The first looks at individuation as an ethical process as Jung understood it. Included in this examination are Jung's philosophical influences and personal experiences, which informed his belief that morality is innate in human beings and rests at the archetypal level of the psyche. Our explorations will also present a classical notion of analytical psychology within the philosophical and psychological contexts of ethics, morality, and conscience, giving us insights into the underpinnings of Jung's theories and ideas. Particular moral and ethical challenges will be highlighted, especially related to conscience and the ethical confrontation with the unconscious. The second part of the book addresses more collective, twenty-first-century implications of Jung's ideas of the "Voice of God." It also explores contemporary issues related to the practice of analytic psychology, given the legacy of Jung's personal relationships with his clients. While supporting individual subjective psychic experience, analysts can side with the psyche to the neglect of collective ethical codes. As a result, many analysts have committed serious boundary violations, all in the name of following the "Voice of God" or the Self. It is possible for an analyst to adhere strictly to collective codes of ethics prescribed by governing bodies and still behave unethically. In this space, the subject of ethics is a much more delicate and ambiguous endeavour. Most of the issues that arise within this area involve non-sexual boundary violations.

As part of this discussion, we will examine the archetypal foundations of analytic boundaries and the important role they play in supporting individuation as an ethical process for both analyst and analysand. I will argue that the therapeutic relationship has an archetypal core that informs our experience of analysis. The constellation of the Divine Healer with its potential to heal also brings with it the potential for the Charlatan and the False Prophet to wound. Central questions within this dynamic are: What is the difference between flexibility and violation? When is the crossing of the boundary experienced as healing by the analysand? When is it experienced as wounding? Case material is provided, which presents both sides of this issue. In conclusion, I look at suffering and the ethical attitudes required to live individuation as an ethical process in everyday life and in our practice.

What is the Heart?

Rumi
(Translated by Coleman Barks)

What is the heart? It is not human,
and it is not imaginary. I call it

you. Stately bird, who one moment
combines with this world, and the

next, passes through the boundary to
the unseen. The soul cannot find you

because you are the soul's wings, how
it moves. Eyes cannot see you: you

are the source of sight. You're the
one thing repentance will not repent,

nor news report. Spring comes: one
seed refuses to germinate and start

being a tree. One poor piece of wood
blackens but it will not catch fire.

The alchemist wonders at a bit of
copper that resists turning to gold.

Who am I that I'm with you and still
myself? When the sun comes up,

the complicated nightmind of the
constellations fades. Snowforms do

not last through July. The heartquality
embodied by our master, Shams

Tabriz, will always dissolve the old
quarrel between those who believe in

the dignity of a human being's decisions
and those who claim they're all illusion.

Part I

ﻊ

Individuation as an Ethical Process

CHAPTER 1

Ethics, Morality and Conscience: Philosophical and Mythological Perspectives

Ultimately, there are but three systems of ethics, three conceptions of the ideal character and the moral life. One is that of Buddha and Jesus which stresses the feminine virtues, considers all men to be equally precious, resists evil only by returning to good, identifies virtue with love, and inclines in politics to unlimited democracy. Another is the ethic of Machiavelli and Nietzsche, which stresses the masculine virtues, accepts the inequality of men, relishes the risks of combat and conquest and rule, identifies virtue with power and exalts a hereditary aristocracy. A third, the ethic of Socrates, Plato and Aristotle, denies the universal applicability of either feminine or masculine virtues; considers that only the informed and mature mind can judge according to diverse circumstance, when love should rule, and when power should rule; identifies virtue therefore, with intelligence, and advocates a varying mixture of aristocracy and democracy in government.

—Will Durant, *The Story of Philosophy*[1]

Since Ancient Grecian times, philosophers have reflected on the intentions and consequences of human behaviour to develop theories of morality and ethics. In the simplest sense, morality and ethics are reflections of the values that sustain and guide us through difficult situations. They do not constitute a rational or scientific argument based on objective data; rather, they are statements of subjective truth that reflect the world view and philosophical orientation of the theorist.

---

1   William Durant, *The Story of Philosophy*, 2nd ed. (New York:. Pocket Books, 1926), p. 137.

The roots of Western philosophical ethical inquiry can be found in Athens in the fifth century BCE. These investigations were important developments in Western civilization and had profound implications. Until that point, an ethos of fate and destiny had governed ancient Greece, holding that every important element was determined by forces beyond individual will or intentions. Greek myths are filled with stories of gods and goddesses who determine the course of human history and oracles who make binding and incontrovertible predictions of future events. In the story of Oedipus, for instance, the hero is impotent to overcome a fate foretold before he was born. Myths like this were part of a society where social position governed the course of the individual's life, traditional customs prescribed social roles, and virtue was based on gender, birth order, and the social standing of one's family. Within this cultural ethos, individual choice and responsibility for one's actions existed in a strange paradox where heroes or heroines were fated to follow a certain path while also freely bringing their fate upon themselves.

During fifth century BCE, Athens was the centre of intellectual life. Sophocles wrote his plays *Oedipus* and *Antigone*, and the plays of Euripides were being performed. At the same time, a broad social and political movement challenged existing norms and social constructs of Greek civilization, eventually shifting the political structure from aristocracy to democracy. Society was questioning the role that fate played in individual lives. A new line of thinking emerged: its proponents contended that if fate was not the governing factor in the pattern of human life, then Eros must play a role. Self-determination meant to follow Eros—to seek that which was most deeply arousing and enlivened the passions.[2] People were then free to follow their desires.

The rise of ethics in ancient Athens can therefore be seen as the result of a culture struggling with the opposing forces of fate and desire. The philosophers Plato, Socrates, and Aristotle were the first to challenge existing moral concepts. They articulated a vision of the human being who had direct responsibility for her own fate and destiny. They explored the concepts of justice, the good life, the characteristics and virtues of a good person, and the origin of "right behaviour." Their solution was to rely on reason and self-mastery—that is, the strength of the ego—to mediate between the power of desires and the will of the gods. Ethics, for the Greeks, was connected to the development of individual moral character and to the practice of virtue.

---

2   John Hanwell Riker, *Ethics and the Discovery of the Unconscious* (Albany, NY : State University of New York Press, 2001), p. 27.

This preoccupation with moral problems has continued to dominate Western thinking. The ethical discourse of the Greeks highlights the duality of spirit and instinct as two opposing but equal forces. The ego's will and power must control and master the instincts. It is the splitting and reinforcing of this duality that has had a tremendous influence on the development of Western philosophy. In contrast, Eastern consciousness has transcended the issue by embracing opposites in one unified whole. We will explore this important distinction in Chapter 2, where we examine Jung's view of individuation and of *Tao* as the unifier of opposites. In this chapter, we will investigate various perspectives on ethics, morality, virtues, and values—religious, philosophical, mythological, and psychological. This subject matter is vast and complex, but it is important to place Jung's ideas of morality, conscience, and the ethical confrontation with the unconscious within a certain context.

Definitions

Before entering into this discussion of the nature of morality and ethical attitude, some terms should be defined.

In academic circles, ethics is the investigation of standards of conduct, human values, the questions of right and wrong, the religious views of good and evil, and how these matters can be expressed in life. Traditional philosophical definitions characterize ethics as a rational system of support for moral conduct through the dynamic examination of human conduct in the context of ideal standards and values. We commonly think of ethics as standards of conduct based on the stated values and norms of behaviour by some collective entity.

Professor of Philosophy Simon Blackburn suggests that the study of ethics attempts to "understand the springs of motivation, reason and feeling that move us. . . . [It] is an enterprise of self-knowledge."[3] Jungian analyst Hester McFarland Solomon suggests that ethics implies an attitude achieved through judgement, discernment and conscious struggle, often between conflicting rights or duties.[4]

It is in this latter definition that we find the connection to Jung's theories of the psyche and psychological development. Ethics or the exploration of what is

---

3   Simon Blackburn, *On Being Good: A Short Introduction to Ethics* (Oxford: Oxford University Press, 2001), p. 5.
4   Hester McFarland Solomon, "The Ethical Self," in *Jungian Thought in the Modern World* (London: Free Association Press, 2001), p. 191.

ethical is a relational and dynamic discussion between competing or conflicting duties, values, or rights. It is a subject that naturally embodies the meaning of the phrase "tension of the opposites"—a term coined by Jung to express a relationship usually involving the ego and some "Other." Ethics is an exploration of "right relationship." The idea of "right relationship" comes from Buddhist thought and refers to the appropriate relationship given the circumstance and the context of a situation. It is similar to the Christian Golden Rule: "Do unto others as you would have them do unto you." The pursuit of the "right relationship" to the "Other" could involve the relationship to either an inner factor—such as the irrationality of the unconscious, a powerful instinctual drive, an inner spiritual imperative or value, a collective or religious value—or an outside situation—such as an organizational policy or the values of another person.

Another name for ethics is "moral philosophy" thus the subject of an ethical discussion is morality. Morality describes virtuous (right, good) behaviour and conduct within the context of specific perceptions, beliefs, and practices. "Ethics" and "morality" are terms that can be used interchangeably, but they have important differences in meaning. As discussed above, the term ethical refers to a specific internal attitude that a person brings to a particular situation. The term morality, on the other hand, is commonly used to describe a specific set of principles or rules governing the behaviour of a group of people. Moral beliefs or moral norms are clarified within the context of larger philosophical traditions, theological systems, and collective norms. (It should be made clear that this represents the common use of the terms "morality," "moral beliefs," and "moral norms." According to philosophical thought, however, moral norms can originate from outside the individual, as collective pronouncements about what makes up good or bad behaviour, or from inside, through the expression of individual values.)

Another way to look at the common definition of moral norms is to say that they are moral "oughts" or "shoulds" that embody the highest virtues within a certain system of thought or culture. The system could be any organized collective such as a religion, a nation, an organization, or even a family. Moral norms identify both the highest virtues or ideals of behaviour and the lowest values—that is, behaviour and actions considered unacceptable and abhorrent to the system. Psychologically, the system, whether individual or collective, then pushes these undesirable behaviours into the Shadow.

James Q. Wilson[5] suggests that a code word for "virtue" and "morality" is value. The dictionary defines "value" as a standard by which individuals judge

5   James Q. Wilson, *The Moral Sense* (New York: The Free Press, 1993).

what is worthwhile, important, and good. Values therefore provide the foundation upon which moral behaviour and actions rest. Values express something basic about an individual's definition of what is important. The way that children learn to identify and define values is a central question in studies of moral development. Values also reflect the ethos of a particular culture or organizational system. Discussions in newspapers or on television are filled with phrases such as "Christian values" and "family values." Values contain implicit moral statements that determine the ways people relate to others and to the world. As in any collective, individuals within a given value system conform to its values rather than developing their own. When individuals develop their own values that oppose collective values, a problem arises. Jung called this a "conflict of duty."

Determining the value of something is the task of the ego's judging function. Jung called it the "feeling function," and, in his discussion of psychological types, he placed this function on the rational axis of psychological consciousness. Here is his definition of feeling: "Feeling is primarily a process that takes place between the ego and a given content, a process, moreover, that imparts to the content a definite value in the sense of acceptance or rejection, 'like' or 'dislike'."[6] William Willeford, in his book *Feeling, Imagination and Self*, believes there may be a deeper origin. "Feeling," he writes, "is the name for the psychic process essential to this knowledge of one's individual essence and its reaching out into the world of others."[7] As these two definitions suggest, the feeling function has multiple aspects. It is related to one's essence, it represents a connection to the Self (the centre of the personality), and it is part of a person's integrity. These are all part of the ethical equation.

The word conscience comes from the Latin *conscientia*. It means "joint knowledge" or "knowledge that we share with others." In various types of historical literature, the word has also been synonymous with "consciousness" or "awareness." This is the way the Stoic philosopher Cicero understood the concept—consciousness of the morality of one's deeds. Conscience is the human ability or faculty that determines whether there is a discrepancy between ego thoughts, behaviour, and words, and a moral ideal or value. Conscience evaluates the moral quality of those thoughts, behaviours, and words, and gives humans the ability to distinguish between "being human" and "being

---

6   C.G. Jung, *Psychological Types*, Vol. 6 of *The Collected Works* (Princeton, NJ: Princeton University Press, 1971), paragraph 724.

7   William Willeford, *Feeling, Imagination and Self* (Evanston, IL.: Northwestern University, 1987).

inhuman." As an expression of morality, conscience is superior to ego wishes, desires, and interests. Ernst Blum suggests that conscience "directs itself to something in us, against something, and we have constantly to direct ourselves in relation to our conscience. It exercises a directing function and causes us to orient ourselves to something."[8] It seems, therefore, that conscience is a form of knowledge that tells us when we are facing an ethical or moral issue. As Jung argued, it is a psychological function and to the extent that the experience of conscience and the knowledge of morality and ethics are shared universally, one could conclude that these phenomena are archetypal.

Moral philosophers agree that the dictates of morality are superior to, and take precedence over, ego self-interest. Morality includes the consideration of an obligation to some "Other," and when we make moral decisions, determining what we "ought" to do, we take into account the demands of conscience. Conscience informs us that a conflict exists between ego self-interest and the "Other" by creating a psychological state of ambivalence. Such can exist at many different levels: between competing instincts and desires; between beliefs, ideas, and attitudes of an individual toward another individual; between groups; or between nations. The conflict becomes an ethical or moral issue when the parties involved have no guidance about what to do or how to behave in a particular circumstance.

Morality and Judeo-Christian Religion

Religion and spirituality have arisen from the aspiration in the human psyche to find meaning and to order the chaos of the world. In all theological traditions, religion has had some foundation in ethics. Like philosophy, religion reflects a particular approach to life within a specific set of integrated belief systems about the nature of the world, of human beings, and of moral conduct. The history of Christian morality is two thousand years old, and thinking in this area has developed different forms, depending on the socio-political environment within which theologians were writing.

Until the Enlightenment in the late 1700s, little distinction was made between ethics and religion. The separation of the two related largely to socio-political realities associated with centuries of religious strife. Much war and immorality had taken place in the name of religious conviction, and the result was religious scepticism. Many have argued that the Enlightenment's

---

8   Ernst Blum, "Freud and Conscience," in *Conscience* (Evanston, IL.: Northwestern University Press, 1970), p. 163.

shunning of religious thought led philosophers to place less importance on conscience and ethical consciousness in philosophy. In a collection of papers published by the C.G. Jung Institute, Zurich, Hans Zbinden writes that "conscience, as historical and psychological experience shows, cannot thrive without religious roots. In time, the decay of faith is followed by the decay of conscience. The connection between them is expressed by the word *religio* which in Latin means not only 'reverence for God' but also ethical conscience."[9]

Within Judeo-Christian religious morality, supreme authority for determining what is or is not a moral act is placed in an all-knowing God. According to the Judeo-Christian myth, the inner voice of conscience and morality has a divine origin: morality starts with God and reflects the very nature of God. Thus, Judeo-Christian views of morality and conscience reflect devotion to a law that exists outside ego consciousness. Early references in the Old Testament place conscience in the context of a divine, omniscient entity—one who knows and evaluates the extent of our morality. Although the Old Testament sometimes presents a wrathful and vengeful Yahweh, God, according to this tradition, is mostly a loving God, reflecting the ideals of human kindness. The ascension of the individual to heaven is predicated on his performing his duty in this life, on earth. Morality therefore existed in relation to the spiritual world, and in relation to the material or instinctual world. An individual's morality determined one's personal salvation. Conscience was the director of the human being's spiritual nature and the inner agent that interpreted divine law.

Early Christian theologians adopted the Jewish belief in personal salvation and accepted the assumption that all human beings possess an inner voice of conscience. It was then the obligation of Christians to discover God's will and to weave it into their daily lives. Conscience was "a witness within all men including pagans; it states what the law of God requires, 'it is the law writing in their hearts' and it accuses all men."[10] Christian theologians adopted the idea that conscience represents an inner voice of divine origin. Therefore, morality becomes consistent with a belief in God, and conscience becomes an internal authority—a gift of God—that is in all human beings. However, as Christian belief evolved, some brands of Christian morality came to exist only in relationship to the spiritual world and not in connection with the material or instinctual worlds. For Christians, if there is no supreme being to lay down the

9   Hans Zbinden, "A Conscience in Our Time," in *Conscience* (Evanston, IL.: Northwestern University Press, 1970), p. 21.

10   Mircea Eliade, *The Encyclopedia of Religion* (New York: MacMillan Publishing Company, 1987), p. 46.

moral law, each individual is free to do as he or she pleases. Without a divine lawgiver, there can be no universal moral law.

According to the teachings of Jesus, as recorded in the New Testament, moral decision making is modelled on the example of Jesus. Christian love as preached by Jesus is *agape* love—based on a certain selflessness that allows people to love others without passing judgement on them. God, in the New Testament, is generous and is believed to be at once fully perfect—entirely holy and righteous—and completely merciful. Philosopher Glenn Tinder suggests that Jesus' *agape* love lies at the core of Christian morality[11] and embodies the value God places on generosity, self-sacrifice, good works, and love not only for one's friends and family but also for one's enemies. It is an ethic of love, forgiveness, and grace that abides by the Golden Rule of doing to others as you would want them to do to you.

Within this system of beliefs, it is thought that human beings are more inclined to do good than to do evil. Good is represented as having an absolute value. It is based on a codifiable and transmittable moral law that comes from a heavenly source and governs the moral affairs of human conduct in a "universal" manner. In their codifiable form, Christian values become a series of moral "oughts," and guilt acts as a signal that a person has failed to abide by them. According to this tradition, evil is excluded from God's realm, but is carried by the Devil, an angel who rebelled against God. It is probably useful at this point to highlight the dualism inherent in the Judeo-Christian system—one which separates God from humans and heaven from earth, pitting these opposites against each other in conflict. Human's dual nature—being good and evil, spiritual and corporeal—is not acknowledged.

Origins of Ethics, Morality, and Conscience: The Debate

Western thought about ethics, morality, and conscience has split in the last three hundred years. With the Enlightenment, thinking concerning these issues becomes characterized by the emergence of scientific rationality and comprised a fundamental change: the origin of morality shifted from God to individual choice and responsibility. A debate concerning the psychic origin of morality has arisen as a result: Do human beings possess a natural and innate (archetypal) morality or are ethics and morality social constructs? Are human beings inherently good, social, and moral as Aristotle suggested? Or

---

11   Glenn Tinder, "Can We Be Good without God?", *The Atlantic Monthly* (December 1989), pp. 65–89.

are human beings, as Freud argued, inherently aggressive and interested above all in their own self-interest? Philosophers and thinkers who believe that the human being is inherently moral also see conscience as an inner function, reflecting an inborn law of Nature. Those who do not believe in this inherent morality define conscience as an outer justice or law—either divine or secular—to which one must sacrifice personal interests. The two positions can be seen in the opposing views of Jung and Freud.

The internationally acclaimed biologist, Edward O. Wilson, delves into this debate in his article "The Biological Basis of Morality."[12] He makes the distinction between transcendentalists, who believe that "moral guidelines exist outside the human mind" (that is, moral values exist independently, whether or not they come from God) and empiricists, who think moral guidelines are "contrivances of the mind" (that is, moral values come from the human being). In psychological terms, the debate he articulates is this: are ethics, moral principles, and conscience products of an innate morality or of universal laws that exist outside ego consciousness, or are they human inventions needed to maintain a society? Transcendentalism, he suggests, finds resonance in the heart, while empiricism wins the mind.

According to Wilson, people with a transcendentalist world view seek to discover universal moral principles that reflect some natural law. Moral reasoning becomes an attempt to validate ethics and to immunize them from doubt and compromise. In this view, ethics are archetypal, either as reflections of God's will or as some other natural universal law. Whether their origin is divine or from some other source, principles exist in the order of Nature, and human beings must discover them. As Wilson suggests:

> In transcendental thinking, the chain of causation runs downward from a given *ought* in religion or natural law through jurisprudence to education and finally to individual choice .... The order of nature contains supreme principles, either divine or intrinsic, and we will be wise to learn about them and find a means to conform to them.[13]

The empiricist world view, Wilson writes, is based on a collective notion of right and wrong embedded in the collective consciousness. It is a voice passed down through the generations, one that has become synonymous with the

---

12   Edward O. Wilson, "The Biological Basis of Morality," *The Atlantic Monthly* (April, 1998), pp. 53–70.

13   *Ibid.*, p. 58.

internalized parent and expressed throughout a society as a code of principles. This perspective places great value on objective scientific knowledge and derives partly from the Greek philosophers Plato and Aristotle, who linked conscience and the expression of morality with rational thought and prudence. Emotions and divine moral principles were left out of the equation. Reason and intellect superseded the irrationality of desire, passion, and the instincts as guides for making moral decisions. The myth of the chariot with two steeds represents Plato's conception of the moral nature. The two steeds represented irrational action coming from the instinctual world, and the charioteer reflected reason. As Enlightenment philosophers began to separate religion from morality, their ethical theories came to be based primarily on reason. Wilson summarizes their orientation this way:

> Strong innate feeling and historical experience cause certain actions to be preferred; we have experienced them, and have weighed their consequences, and agree to conform with codes that express them. Let us take an oath upon the codes, invest our personal honour in them, and suffer punishment for their violation. …. *Ought* is the translation not of human nature but of public will.[14]

A few social biologists are currently investigating the hypothesis that ethical codes arose through an interplay between biology and culture, creating moral or ethical instincts in individuals. Edward O. Wilson suggests that the primary origin of moral instincts lay in the dynamic relationship between cooperation and defection,[15] which arose as a matter of survival collectives and tribes and were cultivated as part of evolution. The essential dilemma seems to have been "Can I get more of what I need—food, sex, shelter, protection, health, money, or power—by cooperating with others or by going it alone?" Wilson suggests that moral development requires a species intelligent enough to judge and manipulate this tension—an ability found only in human beings and possibly higher apes. Among these primates, if cooperation leads to more rewards, then such attitudes and values lead to greater genetic fitness among those who tend to cooperate, who tend to live longer and can pass on their genes through offspring. Wilson gives us this example:

> Imagine a Palaeolithic band of five hunters. One considers breaking away from the others to look for an antelope on his own. If successful, he will

---

14   *Ibid.*
15   *Ibid.*

gain a large quantity of meat and hide—five times as much as if he stays with the band and they are successful. But he knows from experience that his chances of success are low, much less than the chances of the band of five working together. In addition, whether he is successful alone or not, he will suffer animosity from the others for lessening their prospects. By custom, the band members remain together and share equitably the animals they kill. So the hunter stays. He also observes good manners in doing so especially if he is the one who makes the kill. Boastful pride is condemned because it rips the delicate web of reciprocity.[16]

As people have cooperated, their propensity to cooperate has increased. And thus, through several thousand generations, moral instincts or sentiments have arisen and are experienced as conscience, self-respect, remorse, empathy, shame, humility, and moral outrage.

Freud's Superego

Freud's idea of the superego is consistent with an evolutionary model of moral development. In *The Future of an Illusion* (1927), Freud argues that religion undermines the moral responsibility of the individual because he interprets the notion of God within the psyche as an infantile wish for a Father. He argued that the fear of retribution from some unseen supernatural being was not sufficient to induce people to be moral. Rather, mature morality was attained through reason and atheism. Freud's concept of conscience was linked to the Oedipus complex, to the struggle of the ego to grow out of the world of the instincts, and to repression, which he believed was the root of most human suffering. Freud believed that conscience belonged to human beings as a matter of course, but, unlike Jung, he did not think it possessed psychological knowledge. He also did not believe in an innate morality or in a human being's natural inclination to be good. Whatever morality human beings did possess came from learning to repress sexual and aggressive instincts out of fear of losing the love of others and feelings of guilt. Human beings were naturally antisocial and aggressive, and became moral only as a result of civilization.

Conscience, according to Freud, is the function of the "superego"—the inner judge and agency that gives direction to drives, impulses, and instincts, and which reflects the internalization of the father's or parent's authority in the psyche. Acting independently from the ego, the superego works toward some

---

16   *Ibid.*, p. 59.

ego ideal of right and wrong, and speaks to the individual's relationship to the collective—the human community in which he lives. It becomes the internalized voice of the collective. Ernst Blum describes the role of the superego this way:

> The superego is the representative for us of every moral restriction, the advocate of striving toward perfection—it is, in short, as much as we have been able to grasp psychologically of what is described as the higher side of human life. It is the precipitate of everything that parents, teachers and exemplary models have inoculated into us; later this also incarnates the ideals, the moral decencies, the spiritual currents we have absorbed into ourselves.[17]

This view of morality and conscience is connected with the Archetype of the Father and collective moral norms. Jungian analyst Murray Stein calls it a "solar conscience," which is rooted in the patriarchy and in paternal authority. Conscience of this type moves the individual toward holding collective values and aspiring to collective ideals. These ideals of the Father, Authority, and Logos are based on principle, judgment, reason, and rules. Psychologically, it is the Father who introduces the child to the outside world and to the collective, and who imparts societal expectations. Jean Piaget and Lawrence Kohlberg observed the development of solar conscience in children when they investigated how children learn the "rules" of the game. Through exposure to these values, children internalize collective norms by which they later evaluate their behaviour as adults.

Moral and Ethical Instincts: Psychological and Mythological Perspectives

In his book *The Moral Sense*, James Q. Wilson suggests that human beings have a natural moral sense, "a sense that is formed out of the interaction of their innate dispositions with their earliest familial experiences."[18] Our morality is thus an alchemical combination of innate tendencies and our interaction with the collective norms that we internalize when growing up in a particular family and culture. The moral instinct is but one of our human instincts, and it must compete with other instincts, such as the desire to survive, to reproduce,

---

17   Blum, "Freud and Conscience," p. 172.
18   Wilson, *The Moral Sense*, p. 2.

and to accumulate power. The two sides of our nature are at war with each other: instinctual desires and self-interest compete with our need to be social and belong to a community. Through this struggle, we may experience the difference between being human and being inhuman, and the way we resolve it depends on our character, the circumstances of our life, and the socio-political environment in which we live. As Wilson puts it, "To say that people have a moral sense is not the same thing as saying that they are innately good .... But saying that a moral sense exists is the same thing as saying that humans, by their nature, are potentially good."[19]

Wilson believes human beings' natural moral sense, their "an intuitive or directly felt belief about how one ought to act when one is free to act voluntarily,"[20] binds the species together. He has explored four aspects of this moral sense: sympathy, fairness, self-control, and duty. These instincts have their roots in the biological matrix of human beings as social animals and have developed as a result of evolution. This is similar to the hypothesis advanced by Edward O. Wilson, discussed above.

For James Q. Wilson, the moral sense is also related to kinship and to the strong human need for attachment. In other words, morality is based on the values of Eros and the feminine. All human societies are organized around kinship patterns, and the human obligation to kin and to children cannot easily be explained by personal self-interest. It is in the areas of taking care of children and family alliances that one might find the origins of some kind of universality of the moral sense. And it is in the developmental dimension of psychology where the moral sense can be nurtured or deformed because, as Wilson argues, the family has so much influence on the cultivation of morality.

Wilson's arguments about a universal moral sense also come from his observation that common rules within all societies embody the impulse to take care of children and to prohibit incest and unjustifiable homicide. He suggests that these do not constitute universal rules because "what is most likely to be universal are those impulses that, because they are so common, scarcely need to be stated in the form of a rule."[21] Ethical or moral responses, apart from those related to uncommon transgressions like incest and homicide, arise without conscious reflection.

Two Jungian writers provide evidence to support the idea that morality and ethics have an instinctual base and are often experienced viscerally—not

---

19   *Ibid.*, p. 12.
20   *Ibid.*, p. xii.
21   *Ibid.*, p. 18.

only through societal rules. Jungian analyst Robert Bosnak[22] explored the notion of whether human beings, unlike other beings, possess a deep sense that enables us to distinguish between good and bad behaviour. He suggests that such an instinct does exist and that it is felt viscerally—that is, in the body, where we are the most vulnerable. Using the parallel of the body's reaction to foreign physical substances, Bosnak postulates that the psyche has a similar mechanism of revulsion and abhorrence, which rejects actions that we consider alien or foreign to our being. Collective moral codes and systems are therefore built upon the human ability to feel abhorrence and disgust.

Murray Stein's definition of conscience suggests the same visceral response. It is "a gut reaction, and it belongs to the individual. It is not the product of rational thought or reflection. It is an inner agency that speaks for values that are not necessarily identical with the immediate self-interest of the individual."[23] Stein argues that conscience has an instinctive aspect that helps determine our experience of morality. To the degree that it is outside the ego, it acts as an independent complex, which he suggests is rooted in another area of the personality.[24] Stein's ideas concerning the instinctual base of morality are especially relevant because they connect with mythological interpretations of experience.

Greek myths, for instance, were based on a collection of religious beliefs relating to numerous deities. While the moral philosophy of the Greeks was highly rational, the mythology suggested that the world was governed by a instinctual moral laws, as well as physical laws. This instinctual knowledge is a conscience that rests in the archetypal Mother, in the body, in the instincts, and in Nature, rather than in the Father, which, as described above, resides in the superego identified by Freud. Stein has coined the term "lunar conscience" to describe this type of morality. At this level, actions and behaviour are not rational or the product of conscious reflection; they are the result of compulsion, which motivates a person to sacrifice something for a greater good. Stein suggests that morality experienced at this level "transcends the commonly received rules and regulations that govern a specific society."[25]

---

22   Robert Bosnak, "Ethical Instinct" in *Asian and Jungian Views of Ethics* (Westport, CT: Greenwood Press, 1999), pp. 45–63.

23   Murray Stein, *Solar Conscience, Lunar Conscience* (Wilmette, IL: Chiron Publications, 1993), pp. 1–3.

24   Jung's major contribution to this discussion is that conscience is the "Voice of God" within the personality and is thus a reflection of the Self. I will explore this in greater detail in the next chapter.

25   Stein, *Solar Conscience*, p. 55.

Within this mythological moral order are the concepts of fate and hubris. Hubris is arrogance, a lack of humility before the gods. Simply, it is about forgetting that one is human and not divine; it is an archetypal inflation. The punishment for hubris results when an individual has overstepped the boundaries of fate, natural law, and natural development—a cosmic order embodied in the early Greek mother goddesses. This order reflects the "mother right"—that is, a set of obligations that arises from the mother-child relationship. As James Q. Wilson suggests, the morality that lies at the foundation of this natural law arises from a basic need for attachment, love, and Eros and carries with it ideas of connection, embracement, empathy, trust, and feeling. Human beings are subject to natural law because they live within Nature. And in the Greek myths, the violation of those laws produces its own penalties (which arise from the unconscious), such as madness, psychosomatic illness, and personality disorders.

Themis, the Goddess of Justice, probably reflects most clearly the principle of natural law in Greek mythology. As the daughter of Gaia and Uranus, she represents a matriarchal stage of cultural development. Her principal role within the pantheon was to act as an oracle, predicting the future, but she was primarily the voice of the earth and of Nature. Like her mother before her, she acted as the Oracle of Delphi—the same oracle that later became the voice of Apollo. Her name means "right"—but not right in the sense of commandment or decree. Rather, she represented the belief that human beings must remain in "right relationship" with a universal order. Her symbol is the sword, and she stands opposed to hubris. She does not reflect "abstract ideas of righteousness." Instead, her presence in Greek mythology suggests a "development of natural ethics, of a kind of natural righteousness out of the Great Mother."[26] Her other symbols include the lamp and the scales, which are used to weigh the truth of situations. She is also the mother of Horae, of the seasons and hours, and as such, she rules the natural evolution of time and the orderliness of the cosmos. Murray Stein describes how Themis governs hubris:

> While the principle of natural order espoused by Themis is as steady as the earth itself, her specific injunctions are changeable, like the moon. Hubris goes wrong by reversing this: the principle of natural order is ignored and instead of it a specific attitude or ego idealization assumes rigid permanency. Hubris ignores the life situation.[27]

---

26 *Ibid.*, p. 73.
27 *Ibid.*, p. 75.

As Greek mythology moved away from the matriarchal and toward the patriarchal, Themis's role became embodied in social contracts between people, and the instinctual morality she had formerly represented was portrayed through the Erinyes or the Goddesses Nemesis. Erinyes, or the Furies, demand justice and are described as external agencies which punish the individual for violations of the natural moral law. As goddesses of vengeance, they seek those who shed familial blood or break oaths. They defend the rights of "attachment bonds." As Murray Stein writes, they defend

> our intimate and pervasive feelings of attachment, our early physical and psychological bonds of relationship to people and things, and also our bond to our own body and physical need. Lunar conscience takes the attitude a mother takes toward her children: she tends to their physical needs, she loves them unconditionally, emotionally, primitively, absolutely. As a mother would, lunar conscience, recommends that the ego accept life and live it fully. There is imprinted in lunar conscience an ethic of acceptance and of self-acceptance.[28]

In the myths, the Furies erupt suddenly out of the unconscious to plague the ego with their howling. Their most famous victim was Orestes, who violated kinship bonds by killing his mother. His mother had murdered his father, Agamemnon, because he had sacrificed their daughter, Clytemnestra, to secure good winds for a journey to Troy. In his moral dilemma, Orestes consulted Apollo, who at this stage of Greek cultural development was considered to control the Oracle of Delphi. He decrees that Clytemnestra must be executed. Orestes obeys the patriarchal law and does what he is told. Yet afterwards he is driven mad by the voices of the Furies, whom he calls the "bloodhounds of my mother's hate," and he is forced to wander the earth. Psychologically, we experience the Furies as madness, anxiety, or being at the mercy of dark, irrational forces when the consciousness of this "mother right" is lost.

Nemesis is another Greek goddess who personifies retribution for the violation of moral law. Her name means "righteous anger," and her wrath "is directed against those who have violated order, especially the order of nature, and disregarded nature's law and norm."[29] Nemesis turns the wheel of retribution and makes necessary adjustments when the natural order is out of balance.

---

28 *Ibid.*, p. 62.
29 Karl Kerenyi, *The Gods of the Greeks* (New York: Thames and Hudson, 1988), p. 105.

She is also a "time goddess," who was described by Ovid as "the Goddess that abhors boastful words because she brought all kinds and heroes down to destruction in the end, no matter how arrogant they were." Nemesis fights hubris. She was particularly revered by the Stoic philosophers, who saw her as the world-governing principle of Nature.

This expression of a cosmic natural moral order expressed in the Goddess Themis, and the Furies, is also found in other cultures, *Dharma* in the Hindu religion and *Tao* in the Chinese cosmology, for instance. Both reflect Eastern concepts of the natural flow and natural order of the world—concepts that Jung adopted as reflections of the natural flow of the personality and of the world (see next chapter). The Goddess Maat of the older Egyptian civilization represented a similar type of natural order (see Chapter 4).

Moral Relativism

Modern philosophy has largely abandoned the issue of morality as a subject for discussion and has turned its attention toward existentialism and nihilism. In *The Moral Sense*, James Q. Wilson suggests that recent philosophical theories of human behaviour have broken with early philosophical perspectives on morality and that moral relativism has been the result. In the current collective context, no one can agree on specific morals or virtues, and the resulting moral relativism has led people to refrain from passing judgment on the actions of others, basing their views instead on an attitude of tolerance. There is no universal truth or standard by which to measure human behaviour; everything is acceptable within the values of the culture or individual.

Elements of moral relativism can be found in the philosophy of the Greek Sophists. They argued that since there is no universal moral truth, moral law is a construct of society, a human invention based on human needs and desires. Modern moral relativism is based on a purely subjective orientation to ethics, which claims that "everyone has a right to develop their own form of life, grounded in their own sense of what is really important or of value. People are called upon to be true to themselves and to their own self-fulfillment. What this consists of, each must, in the last instance, determine for him or herself. No one else can or should try to dictate its content."[30] Moral standards are therefore relative to something else: culture, a society, a person, or history. As psychologist Stephen J. Freeman writes, "Relativism doesn't tell us which

---

30   Charles Taylor, *The Ethics of Authenticity* (Cambridge: Harvard University Press, 1991), p. 14.

acts are right or wrong (absolutely); rather, it views the characteristics relative to cultural diversity and then describes them (relative to the culture) as being right or wrong."[31]

Moral relativism differs from the archetypal perspective in important ways. If all of humanity needs guidance in terms of specific situations such as dealing with death, institution of property, prohibition against murder, abhorrence of incest, and appropriate relationship to children, we might say that the core of ethics is archetypal. Therefore, ethics are universal in the sense that all cultures have norms or ideals that guide actions and behaviour. However, each culture creates ethics relative to its own situation.

Taken to the extreme, moral relativism becomes subjective, and standards become the product of personal opinion, thoughts, and attitudes. In his book *Ethics: An Introduction to Philosophy and Practice*, Stephen J. Freeman brings clarity to the concept of moral relativism when he draws a distinction between opinion and truth. He points out that the question of

> "... what is mere opinion and what is truth?", is intimately involved in searching for the underpinning of ethics. Ethics seeks reasons or rationale that support one position over another .... But to gain knowledge of the truth we must first distinguish between knowledge and opinion. Socrates said that to know the good is to do the good and to know the good requires that certain conditions be met. They include sufficient reflection and full consent of the will. Sufficient reflection meant that one is fully aware of the gravity of his/her proposed action. Full consent of the will means that the action is taken freely and not under the influence of limiting factors such as force, fear or blinding passion.[32]

Citing Marx and Freud, to name two thinkers who have contributed to modern moral relativism, James Q. Wilson calls attention to the lack of bearings which society currently has for making moral choices: "God is dead or silent, reason is suspect or defective, nature meaningless or hostile. As a result, man is adrift on an uncharted sea, left to find his moral bearings with no compass, no pole start, and so able to do little more than utter personal preferences, bow to historical necessity, or accept social conventions."[33]

---

31 Stephen J. Freeman, *Ethics: An Introduction to Philosophy and Practice* (Belmont, CA: Wadsworth Thomson Learning, 2000), p. 45.

32 *Ibid.*, pp. 38–39.

33 Wilson, *The Moral Sense*, p. 5.

Ethics and the Discovery of the Unconscious

Early seventeenth-century philosophers shifted the onus of moral responsibility from God or a transpersonal authority to human reason and intellect. A century later, philosophers such as Marx and Nietzsche were encountering forces and energy in the world that could overtake individual intentions and will. As a result of these explorations and the "discovery of the unconscious,"[34] new dimensions of human nature were revealed and a new field of psychological study was developed. The early explorers into this mysterious world—Charcot, Janet, and Mesmer—were baffled by illnesses that could not be treated by conventional medical approaches. In his book *The Discovery of the Unconscious*, Henri Ellenberger highlights two prominent figures at the beginning of what he calls "dynamic psychiatry," which would later develop into psychoanalysis and analytical psychology: Johan Joseph Gassner (1727–1779), a priest, was known in Europe for healing people through exorcism, and Franz Mesmer (1734–1815), who developed a method of "extracting" a person's disease through magnets.

It was in the healing professions that the clash between the spiritual dimensions of the psyche and the scientific rationality of the Enlightenment would be played out. With the discovery of the unconscious, the causes of mental illness and neurosis were identified as having their origins in something other than the body. Exorcism of evil spirits, magnetism, and hypnosis were found to be more effective than the rational methods of medical science. The exploration of physically unexplainable diseases continued through the nineteenth century and led to Sigmund Freud's development of the psychoanalytical method. Freud recognized that people experience inexplicable psychic events such as dreams, slips of the tongue, forgetfulness, and other behaviours that seem quite resistant to any attempt to change them; human will power was limited, another agent or force outside the realm of consciousness was at work.

John Hanwell Riker,[35] a professor of Philosophy at Colorado College, suggests that the recognition of such a large and pervasive force outside of our conscious awareness is cause for rethinking ethics. Many of the rational scien-

---

34   The title of this section, "Discovery of the Unconscious," comes from two books: John Hanwell Riker's *Ethics and the Discovery of the Unconscious* and Henri Ellenberger's *The Discovery of the Unconscious.*

35   John Hanwell Riker, *Ethics and the Discovery of the Unconscious* (Albany: State University of New York Press, 1997).

tific views of ethics discussed earlier are based on the assumption that human beings have the ability to direct their lives and to take full responsibility for their values and their actions. Ethical positions assume that individuals can become aware of all the forces that affect them and make informed decisions. These theories assume that individuals are free to control their actions and are therefore responsible for the choices they make. The presence of the unconscious, with its powerful effect on our perceptions and actions, challenges this notion of responsibility and the ability of the ego to make completely informed choices. Jung explained the unconscious as a "living psychic entity which, it seems, is relatively autonomous, behaving as it was a personality with intentions of its own." The implications of this statement for ethical codes, ethical committees, and the legal system are significant.

Our perceptions of the ethical orientation of the individual are also challenged when the effects of the unconscious are taken into account. Primarily through the work of Jung, we now have an understanding of these effects. The personal unconscious contains material that we either forget or repress because it is too painful or hurtful. Material in the personal unconscious can also contain information that we perceived subliminally during the day but did not actively register. Jung also identified a "collective unconscious", the deepest and most primitive level of the unconscious, where archetypes originate. Contents of the collective unconscious reflect material that is typical of human behaviour which can never be brought to consciousness. All of these levels of the unconscious have the potential to pull ego consciousness into their field. The more deeply unconscious the material is, the less the will has the power to fight its effects. The ethical attitude then takes on a different slant and must assume a stance of mediation. Jungian analyst Adolf Guggenbühl-Craig describes it this way: "Morality is the ego's heroic attempt to find rules for the relationship of archetypes among themselves, for our relationship to our fellow humans, and for our relationship to our environment as a whole."[36]

ॐ

In recent centuries, these explorations of ethics, morality, and conscience have touched on two poles of thinking: the empiricist or evolutionary biological view, which takes a rational approach to the presence of morality in society, arguing that it is a human invention, necessary for living harmoniously with others, and the transcendentalist view, which states that there are innate

---

36   Adolf Guggenbühl-Craig, *The Emptied Soul: On the Nature of the Psychopath* (Woodstock, NY: Spring Publications, 1999), p. 98.

moral laws, whether these laws come from God or some natural source. Jung's descriptions of archetypes and his thoughts on ethics, morality, and conscience embraced both empiricism and transcendentalism on a number of different levels. These explorations will be the subject of our next chapter.

CHAPTER 2

Jung's Exploration of Morality and Conscience

Whoever is incapable of this moral resolution, of this loyalty to himself, will never be relieved of his neurosis. On the other hand, whoever is capable of it will certainly find the way to cure himself.[1]

—C.G. Jung

As we saw in the previous chapter, the psychological function of ethics has both instinctual and spiritual components. The debate that biologist Edward O. Wilson highlights—between science and religion and between the empiricist and the theologian/philosopher—is particular relevant to Jung because of the latter's theory of archetypes. Archetypes, Jung suggests, are "typical modes of apprehension"[2]—that is, patterns of psychic perception and understanding common to all human beings—and have what he characterized as "infrared" and "ultraviolet" poles. Believing that archetypal representations could be symbolically placed on either end of the colour spectrum, Jung situated the biologically-driven instincts at the infrared end of the spectrum and archetypal representations (images or spiritual perceptions) at the ultraviolet end, as he felt that violet had a mystical quality. In his early work, Jung theorized that instincts were different from archetypes, in that they were "typical modes of action."[3] His early ideas of the archetype were based on the view that spirit was split from matter—a conception that originated from his association with Freud.

---

1   C.G. Jung, *Two Essays in Analytical Psychology*, Vol. 7 of *The Collected Works* (Princeton, NJ: Princeton University Press, 1966), paragraph 498.

2   C.G. Jung, *The Structure and Dynamics of the Psyche*, Vol. 8 of *The Collected Works* (Princeton NJ: Princeton University Press, 1969), paragraph 280.

3   *Ibid.*, paragraph 273.

As Jung later developed his theory of archetypes in *On the Nature of the Psyche* (1947)[4], his thinking changed so that the polarity presented in his early thinking (1919) was transformed into a continuum and symbolized by the entire colour spectrum. He now considered archetypes to be both spiritual (that is, about images) and instinctual (i.e., arising in nature and in the body).

Jung's own life can be seen as an attempt to integrate what he called "Personality No. 1," the scientist, the empiricist who lived according to the "Spirit of the Times," with "Personality No. 2," the philosopher, theologian and mystic who valued and worked with the "Spirit of the Depths." He embodied this polarity from a very young age. Consciously, he identified with the scientist and was attracted to the nature of scientific facts and truths based on research and observation. But these could not provide him with meaning about what he considered the true reality of the world. Through the study of religion and philosophy, however, he could explore issues of spirituality, spiritual problems, and the deeper questions of life. This might explain why he coined new psychological words for what theologians have described as spiritual experiences for centuries. It is possible that he resisted this label of mystic in an attempt to gain credibility for his ideas.

In this chapter, we will look at Jung's ideas of morality, conscience, and the "ethical problem of individuation," which are in evidence throughout the *Collected Works*. We will also look at Jung's personal experiences that informed these ideas—experiences that demonstrated what he called the "ethical confrontation with the unconscious."[5] His views were deeply influenced by the rational thinking embodied in Enlightenment philosophy and by Christian theology. For instance, he subscribed to an idea that was pioneered by Enlightenment philosophers: that each individual human had an original way of being in the world. He also synthesized the scientific and theological poles of the ethical question in his concept of the "Voice of God," in that this notion embodied an obvious theological perspective that could be apprehended by scientific and empirical means of observation.

In his psychological writing, Jung intuitively synthesized three basic systems of ethics, described by philosopher Will Durant in the quotation at the beginning of Chapter I. One system favours the feminine values of Eros and equates virtue with love. The second emphasizes the masculine qualities of

---

4   C.G. Jung. *The Structure and Dynamics of the Psyche*, Vol. 8 of *The Collected Works* (Princeton, NJ: Princeton University Press, 1969).

5   Most of his personal material is taken from his autobiography *Memories, Dreams, Reflections*, supplemented by material from Deirdre Bair's *Jung: A Biography*.

combat and rules and equates virtue with power. The third, originating with the Greek philosophers Socrates, Plato, and Aristotle, says that only an informed and mature mind (the ego) can mediate between the masculine and the feminine. All three perspectives are contained in Jung's philosophy and psychology, where they are synthesized into a fourth perspective—that of wholeness.

Jung's Western Influences

Childhood

Jung's childhood was dominated by religious discussions and sermons, thanks to a predominance of parsons and ministers in his immediate family, so it is not surprising that from an early age Jung was preoccupied with the idea of God. At the same time, he was filled with doubt and many questions. When he was eleven years old, Jung had a vision that became the catalyst for a life-long search for the true nature of God. In this vision, Jung saw God letting go an "enormous turd which falls upon the sparkling new roof, shatters it, and breaks the walls of the cathedral."[6] He describes many years later in *Memories, Dreams, Reflections* that the experience was both illuminating and shaming. It was illuminating because he recognized that it was an experience of a living god. He also suspected that there was a terrible, dark side to God. He dared not speak of the vision to anyone because of his shame. He tried to will himself not to see the image but to no avail. He was sure that, according to Church doctrine, he would be condemned to eternal damnation for even considering something that diverged from orthodox theology. He felt that this knowledge fated him to loneliness and isolation.

Jung writes about the spiritual angst and trouble he felt when listening to the emotional sermons of his father about an all-good God. He had little opportunity to question that Christian belief, however, and discussions with his father in late adolescence left Jung feeling unsatisfied. His father responded to his questions by saying, "One ought not to think but to believe."[7]

The image that Jung witnessed in his imagination fascinated and intrigued him enough to lead him on a search for the nature of the secret. He says it was a crucial time in his life, when he felt that he had to take responsibility for his own fate. Having encountered an image of suffering, imperfection, and evil that was different from what he had been taught, he had to find a reason for the apparent contradiction. As a way to escape the bickering of his parents

---

6   C.G. Jung, *Memories, Dreams, Reflections* (New York: Random House, 1961), p. 40.
7   *Ibid.*, p. 43.

and because he believe that he was being asked to think about these things, Jung began using his father's library for research about the nature of God. At first he poured through the family bible, but found nothing that answered his questions. However, he was convinced that there were people in the world who were looking at these issues rationally, and he continued to search for them.

At the suggestion of his mother, Jung read Goethe's *Faust*, which introduced him to a world where the devil and evil were not dismissed but were taken seriously as sources of suffering. The library also contained a philosophical encyclopaedia. Philosophers could not prove that God existed; instead, they claimed that "god" was an idea engendered in the minds of humans. At its worst, "god" was merely an arbitrary abstraction.

Jung read Pythagoras, Heraclitus, Empedocles, Plato, Meister Eckhart, and St. Thomas of Aquinas but could find no insight into the darker sides of God's nature. He viewed their explanations as mostly lifeless and as "tricks of logic" because they were trying to prove a belief through logical arguments. Jung, on the other hand, was searching for something that could help him come to terms with his own subjective experience. His dissatisfaction with abstractions and theory was consistent throughout his life. It was particularly acute in the area of morality and ethics, where he was more interested in empirical and practical approaches.

Schopenhauer

Jung found that the ideas of Schopenhauer were more satisfying than those of other philosophers. "Here at last," he wrote, "was a philosopher who had the courage to see that all was not for the best in the fundaments of the universe."[8] Schopenhauer questioned the Christian all-good and all-wise God, as well as the harmony of the cosmos. In his principal book, *The World as Will and Representation*, Jung later recognized a new definition of God. Schopenhauer's articulation of Nature's cruelty supported Jung's own experience and his doubt in the natural goodness or decency of human beings. Jung writes: "I knew myself well enough to know that I was only gradually, as it were, distinguishing myself from an animal."[9] With his inherently pessimistic philosophy, Schopenhauer saw life as evil and pain, and identified relief from suffering as the basic stimulus for human activities. This image of the world likely resonated deeply with Jung's vision of God's turd. While Jung found a reflection of his own experience in Schopenhauer's sombre views, he felt that

---

8   *Ibid.*, p. 69.
9   *Ibid.*

the philosopher's solutions to the problems of the world were inadequate and inconsistent. However, his explorations of Schopenhauer's philosophy led him to Immanuel Kant.

Kant

In *Memories, Dreams, Reflections*, Jung makes only a few references to Kant and his influence on him, but he does say that his ideas "brought about a revolutionary alteration" of his attitude to the world and to life.[10] It is in this philosopher that Jung found the notion of the *a priori*—universal, pre-existing principles in the psyche. Another way of describing the *a priori* is to say "innate" or "before experience," but Jung described these principles as *archetypes*. According to Kant's belief in free will in the face of moral decisions, the ego had ultimate power to know and to will morality and moral law. It is possible that this idea contributed to Jung's belief in the ego's role of discrimination and evaluation in the ethical confrontation with the unconscious.

Kant's philosophy was based on the idea of universal moral imperatives, but it had a practical and rational implementation, as he believed that religion was the practical expression of morality. He placed both concepts beyond reason and believed that morality must be derived from the inner self by direct perception and intuition."[11] For Kant, as for Jung, knowledge was derived directly from experience. Kant described the moral sense as a reflection of a universal law of nature that allows humans to know what is right and what is wrong. We experience this knowledge through the phenomenological manifestations of the universal moral law in our immediate feelings—not through our reason. "The moral law in our hearts," according to Kant, "is unconditional and absolute."[12] It is a function of belief and faith. Kant's "good" action is not judged by its results but by whether it is done in accordance with our own inner sense of duty to this universal moral law, which exists *a priori* and is therefore independent of and pre-existent to all human behaviour.[13]

At the same time, Kant was a supporter of the ideas of the Enlightenment that saw the rise of science, the separation of God from Creation, and a disjunction between religion and morality. He advocated a rational theology, and

---

10   Jung is reported as writing to a student at the C.G. Jung Institute that Kant was "his philosopher," as quoted in Sonu Shamdasani, *Jung and the Making of Modern Psychology: The Dream of a Science* (p. 168).

11   Will Durant, *The Story of Philosophy*. (New York: Pocket Books, 1926) p. 276.

12   *Ibid.*

13   Kant's Practical Imperative, which states that individuals are not to treated merely as a means to an end, is the cornerstone for the current code of ethics of the profession.

assigned to human beings the freedom to rise above instinctual existence to create their own fates. He asserted that human beings have free will, and it is this freedom that provides the ground for moral concepts.

Nietzsche

Jung studied Nietzsche's philosophy in university and possibly had a secret fear that he was very much like Nietzsche in his preoccupation with madness and the dark side of the psyche. He was impressed by the philosopher's brilliance—though he also found his ideas "morbid."[14] It was not until after his break with Freud in 1912 that Jung delved into Nietzsche's writings again. He discovered that he shared a great deal with Nietzsche, including being "haunted by Christianity." In his Introduction to the *Seminar on Nietzsche's* Zarathustra, Professor Emeritus of Philosophy at the University of California, James Jarrett, suggests that Jung found in Nietzsche an illustration of his position that "one's most basic beliefs have their roots in personality."[15] Jung also found that the philosopher's interests were more psychological than metaphysical.

> In the semi-legendary Persian Prophet Zarathustra, he [Nietzsche] found his spokesman for the necessity of a complete reversal of mankind's attitudes, beliefs, and aspirations. Everything that has been revered—especially by Christians—was to be denounced and abandoned, and that which had been reviled was to be embraced, and practised. In what he called the "transvaluation of all values," he celebrated not amoralism but what the western tradition has called immoralism and immorality.[16]

Speaking of Jung and Nietzsche, Jarrett suggests that:

> Theirs alike was a philosophy of darkness, no less than light, a celebration of the Dionysian spirit wherein is found the scariness of the unconscious with its alarming dreams which are yet the great source of human creativity.[17]

---

14 Jung. *Memories, Dreams, Reflections*, p. 102.
15 James L. Jarrett, ed., *Jung's Seminar on Nietzsche's* Zarathustra (Princeton, NJ: Princeton University Press, 1998), p. xiii.
16 *Ibid.*, p. xvii.
17 *Ibid.*, p. xx.

Jung's Eastern Influences

According to J.J. Clarke in *Jung and Eastern Thought*,[18] Jung's explorations of Eastern philosophy and thinking can be traced to his reading of Schopenhauer and other German philosophers. These thinkers looked to the East as they examined their assumptions about Western civilization. Confucian thought, with its emphasis on the integration of ethical, political, and cosmological ideas, particularly fascinated Enlightenment philosophers. They were attracted to the rationalist moral philosophy that lay at the foundation of Confucian thought, and to the absence of divine revelation of omnipotent law and dogma that dominated Christian theology. As a result, Confucius was revered as the ideal philosopher–statesman.

Jung's introduction to Eastern philosophy later sparked his study in comparative religion, where he found a resolution to his moral conflict with Christian theology. Eastern religions confront the paradox of life and recognize the tension of good and evil within moral decisions. In Chinese philosophy, good exists simultaneously with evil, as does light with dark. In these opposites, the whole can be seen, along with the third–or synthesizing– principle that contains them both and represents a latent possibility. This third principle is a reflection of the individuation path, or the "middle way," which embraces the polarities of good and evil, light and dark.

The cosmological vision expressed in Chinese philosophy is strongly influenced by the early Chinese folk religion, which is now called Taoism. Along with the collective philosophy of Confucianism, these two systems share a common set of metaphysical terms and cosmological principles, a fundamentally optimistic view of human nature, and a belief in the innate and positive ethical potential of human beings. Confucianism prescribed a clear order of social and family relationships based on kinship and ancestor worship rooted in patrilineal descent and in patriarchal authority. Returning to Murray Stein's distinction between solar conscience and lunar conscience (described in the previous chapter), Confucianism superficially reflects a solar conscience, an adherence to outward and collective values—the Chinese version of Freud's superego. Because Jung differed with Freud regarding the moral importance of the superego and collective values, placing more importance on morality derived from the inner self, it is not surprising that Jung does not appear to have been interested in Confucianism. (His references to this philosophy are rare in the *Collected Works*.) On the other hand, ideas related to Taoism greatly

---

18   J.J. Clarke, *Jung and Eastern Thought* (London: Routledge, 1994).

influenced his theories. Jung tended to see Taoist thought as typical of Chinese thinking, although this is not the case. The two traditions—Taoism and Confucianism—are deeply connected in Chinese thinking and contain both solar and lunar aspects of ethical questions.

Confucian Morality

Confucian ethics originated with the Chinese philosopher, teacher, and social and ethical reformer Confucius (551–479 BCE). Concentrating on the collective norms and customs of his day, his ideas arose in response to the chaos of the Chou Dynasty (1100–600 BCE). During this time, also known as the Warring States Period, the ancient Chinese feudal system was disintegrating and the country was in disarray. As a means of restoring order to this environment of political upheaval, Confucius developed a systematic and rationalistic moral doctrine that governed familial relationships and the relationship of the individual to ancestors, family, and society. The Confucian system influenced Chinese culture for two thousand years.

Confucius believed that individuals had an innate moral disposition called *jen*. This concept existed as a principle before the philosopher's time, but it became central to Confucian moral philosophy. Literally translated, *jen* means "humanity," "human heartedness," "justice," "compassion," "love," or "virtue."[19] Not only did the principle of *jen* express an ideal in terms of human relationships, it also contained a transcendental principle, for it was seen as the heart's divinity and connected to the path of self-realization and our true nature. *Te*, according to Confucian thought, was a positive moral force that derived from Heaven. In Confucius' Analects, *te* is referred to as a morally authenticating power, or moral character. Much of Confucian thought rests on the cultivation of *te*, morality, and ethical decision making. Stephen McFarlane, a specialist in Chinese religion and philosophy, suggests that Confucian morality did not merely counsel people to follow collective rules, it called for a higher differentiation in ethical decision-making that was aligned with an appropriate reverence for the sacred.

> Conscious decision-making and consequentialist thinking would have been regarded as a lower or preliminary stage of ethical development. The morally accomplished sage or exemplary person would not be in "two minds." Moral decision making and the imposition of externally con-

---

19   S. Ma, "Jung and the Chinese Way," in *Psychology and Religion at the Millennium and Beyond* (Tempe, AZ: New Falcon Publications, 1998), p. 59.

straining moral rules are actually seen as features of a preliminary and immature stage of moral development. At a more advanced stage of moral development, the Confucian sage would be at ease and unconstrained in his behaviour, yet he acts appropriately and in accord with *li*.[20, 21]

Confucius' moral philosophy was developed and refined by Mencius (374–289 BCE), whose ideas will be discussed in Chapter 4 on the Heart.

Taoism

The basis of the Chinese cosmological view is the connection between the microcosm of the individual and the macrocosm of society and the universe. It is a symbolic and holistic perspective, rooted in the principles of Taoism. *Tao* means "the Way," "the power," "the path," "principle," "doctrine," or "system of order," and is seen as a dynamic energy force that permeates all things. *Tao* is divided into two fundamentally opposing principles, contained within the *Yin Yang* symbol.

The principle of *Yin* and *Yang* gives rise to all existence and governs all change and all life. Behind the bewildering multiplicity and contradictions of the world lies a single unity, the *Tao*. The purpose of human life, then, is to live life according to the *Tao*, which requires passivity, calm, non-striving (*wu wei*), humility, and lack of planning, for to plan is to go against the *Tao*. Ancient Taoists sought to find evidence of *Tao* within themselves and in patterns of events within the natural and social worlds, and to master a union between their nature and life.

Taoism and the *Tao Te Ching* are said to have originated with Lao Tzu about 604 BCE. The *Tao Te Ching* is the classic book about integrity and the Way, and sits at the foundation of Chinese spiritual discourse. Philosophically, the concept of *Tao* has influenced much of Chinese art and science.

Early Taoists criticized Confucian thought for its conservatism and rigidity, and disagreed with its concept of *te* as a morally authenticating power or moral character. Lao Tzu believed that *te* was so integral and natural to human beings that to cultivate it or instruct it would, in fact, injure it.[22] He suggested that the imposition of external rules and constraints obscures individual innate

---

20 *Li* is the term for ritual action and is used in connection with formal rites and sacrifices correctly performed.

21 Stewart McFarlane, "Chinese and Japanese Religions," in *Making Moral Decisions* (London: Pinter Publishers, Ltd., 1994), p. 171.

22 *Ibid.*

moral sense. Since people would then tend to rely on the rules, rather than their own innate moral power, chaos would result when situations arose where the rules were inapplicable. Lao Tzu therefore rejects the Confucian establishment and values, and sees them as causes of moral weakness. Verse 18 of the *Tao Te Ching* articulates this beautifully:

> When the Great *Tao* was abandoned,
> There appeared humanity and justice.
> When intelligence and wit arose,
> There appeared great hypocrites.
>
> When the six relations lost their harmony,
> There appeared filial piety and paternal kindness.
> When darkness and disorder began to reign in a kingdom,
> There appeared loyal ministers.[23]

In his translation of the *Tao Te Ching*, Victor Mair defines *te* as "integrity." Early texts of the book from the Chou period (1100–600 BCE) convey its meaning as "character," "intentions," "disposition," "personal strength," and "worth." It is the sum total of one's actions and reflects the moral weight of an individual. "In short, *te* is what you are. *Te* represents self-nature or self-realization only in relation to the cosmos. It is in fact the actualization of the cosmic principle of the self. *Te* is the embodiment of the Way and is the character of all entities in the universe. Each creature, each object has a *te* which is its own manifestation of *Tao*."[24]

Jung's Views on Morality

The journey that Jung took to seek an explanation for his vision of God's turd created a framework that can help us understand his views of morality and conscience. Like ancient Chinese thinkers, Jung believed that morality was innate within the human psyche and that it was central to the task of being human in modern times, although he did not dismiss the collective aspect of ethics, recognizing that it also provided the foundation for a collective moral code. Morality arose from holding the tension of the opposites, which he

---

23   Lao Tzu, *Tao Te Ching*, trans. John C.H. Wu (Boston: Shambhala, 1989), p. 37.
24   Victor Mair, *Commentary on Lao Tzu's* Tao Te Ching (New York: Bantam Books, 1990), p. 135.

equated with following our own natural life path. As he wrote in 1916:

> Morality is not imposed from outside; we have it in ourselves from the
> start—not the law, but our moral nature without which the collective life
> of human society would be impossible. That is why morality is found at all
> levels of society. It is the instinctive regulator of action which also governs
> the collective life of the herd.[25]

In *Psychological Types*, written eight years later, the influence of Taoist
philosophy on his view of morality is even more explicit. Here, he describes
morality as being in alignment with the flow of psychic energy:

> Morality is inherent in the laws of life and fashioned like a house or a
> ship or any other cultural instrument. The natural flow of libido, this same
> middle path, means complete obedience to the fundamental laws of human
> nature, and there can positively be no higher moral principle than harmony
> with natural laws that guide the libido in the direction of life's optimum.[26]

For Jung, the natural laws of the human psyche were also "the path of
our destiny and the law of our being."[27] The ultimate ethical task was consciousness, becoming aware of ourselves and our motivations. This concept of
the path is closely linked to Jung's theory of the natural flow of libido, which
also means the middle path, the right, the good, and moral order. Moreover,
this theory is very similar to the Eastern concept of the realization of *Tao*,
the discovery of our innate morality through the synthesis that results from
the conflict of opposites. Jung wrote that "the aim of Taoist ethics is to find
deliverance from the cosmic tension of the opposites and to return to *Tao*."[28]
Jung also used this concept to explain the light and dark aspects of archetypal
theory. *Tao* was the stream of integrity that transcended the archetypes and
their drive for dominance.

Jung's core belief is that individuation—the innate drive within everyone
toward wholeness—is connected to morality. *Tao* is personality, or the Self,

---

25   C.G. Jung, *Two Essays in Analytical Psychology*, Vol. 7 of *The Collected Works* (Princeton,
　　NJ: Princeton University Press, 1966), paragraph 30.
26   C.G. Jung, *Psychological Types*, Vol. 6 of *The Collected Works* (Princeton, NJ: Princeton
　　University Press, 1971), paragraph 355.
27   *Ibid.*
28   *Ibid.*, paragraph 370.

the guiding function of the psyche. Since morality has to do with living in harmony with the natural laws of our own individual natures, we are moral when we align with this nature and our inner flow of life. As Jungian analyst John Beebe puts it, "for Jung, *Tao* was the ground of integrity."[29]

Jung was also concerned with the origin of moral laws within the psyche and with the origin of deviation from them. He identified this conflict of duty as the "chief cause of neurosis."[30] It is a collision that originates in the conflict with one's Self—with one's own inner moral law. Jung's conflict of duty began with his vision of God's turd falling on Basel Cathedral—an impression of God that could not be reconciled with what Jung had understood of Christianity. Sonu Shamdasani suggests that this experience gave Jung "a direct immediate experience of the living God"[31] and launched a sense of responsibility to find his own way. Jung would later come to believe that these difficult moral issues could not be answered by the collective, and that resolution had to come from somewhere within the individual:

> If a man is endowed with an ethical sense and is convinced of the sanctity of ethical values, he is on the surest road to a conflict of duty. And although this looks desperately like a moral catastrophe, it alone makes possible a higher differentiation of ethics and a broadening of consciousness. A conflict of duty forces us to examine our conscience and therefore to discover the Shadow. This, in turn, forces us to come to terms with the unconscious.[32]

According to Jung, psychological suffering and neurosis are symptoms of ethical dilemmas that cannot be resolved by the collective or outer moral law but through moral loyalty to oneself. Jung's conflict of duty launched his own individuation process—and his lifelong exploration of the nature of the psyche and of divinity was the path through which he found meaning and alleviated his neurotic suffering. He wrote: "Whoever is incapable of this moral resolution, of this loyalty to himself, will never be relieved of his neurosis. On the other hand, whoever is capable of it will certainly find the way to cure himself."[33]

---

29   John Beebe, *Integrity in Depth* (New York: Fromm Publishing, 1995), p. 28.

30   C.G. Jung. "Foreword to Neumann: *Depth Psychology and the New Ethic*" in *The Symbolic Life*, Vol. 18 of *The Collected Works* (Princeton NJ: Princeton University Press, 1949), paragraph 1408.

31   C.G. Jung. Introduction to *The Red Book*, p. 194

32   *Ibid.*, paragraph 1417.

33   Jung, *Two Essays on Analytical Psychology*, paragraph 498.

A full expression of Jung's thoughts on this issue can be found in two articles that he wrote when he was more than eighty years old: "Good and Evil in Analytical Psychology" (1959) and "A Psychological View of Conscience" (1958).

Good and Evil

Inherent in Jung's concept of the tension of the opposites are the moral opposites of "good and evil." He discusses these ideas at several points in the *Collected Works* but mainly in the 1959 article, "Good and Evil in Analytical Psychology." In exploring good and evil, Jung says two things: first, that good and evil are archetypal principles; second, that whatever we consider to be evil is based on a subjective judgement or a value held by the individual—a judgement that cannot be objectively defended, for another person may make a different judgement.

The ultimate judge of what is good or evil is unknowable, and as Christian theologians and Edward O. Wilson's transcendentalists believe, "to see through a concrete situation to the bottom is God's affair alone."[34] In this, Jung's thinking harmonizes with that of Christian theologians. Jung points out that the word "principle" derives from a word meaning "beginning," and that the ultimate principle is God. "Good and evil are principles of our ethical judgment," he writes, "but, reduced to their ontological roots, they are 'beginnings,' aspects of God, names for God."[35]

The beginning of consciousness for human beings was the knowledge of good and evil. We know this from the Book of Genesis and the expulsion of Adam and Eve from the Garden of Eden after they ate the Apple from the Tree of the Knowledge of Good and Evil. Jung believed that these principles were the catalyst for consciousness, and they entangle us in something that we are left to find our own way out of. This situation marks the beginning of personal ethics, where the individual must confront the Absolute and attempt a path that is condemned by current morality and the guardians of the laws. In this conflict between a person's innermost nature and some outside authority or judge, the individual must seek the middle position of *Tao*, where one is no longer at the mercy of the opposites good and evil. This position is reached through freeing oneself from both and assessing both.

---

34   C.G. Jung, "Good and Evil in Analytical Psychology" in *Civilization in Transition*, Vol. 10 of *The Collected Works* (Princeton NJ: Princeton University Press, 1970), paragraph 862.

35   *Ibid.*, paragraph 864.

A Psychological View of Conscience

In his article "A Psychological View of Conscience," Jung outlines his views of the unconscious authority that ultimately has the final say about moral and ethical conflicts: the "Voice of God". He writes that conscience is a complex phenomenon containing emotional responses and value judgements that drive our actions. These judgements are "grounded on rational feeling," which includes a specific "feeling tone" reaction.[36] It is this reaction that indicates that there is a conflict or something is out of alignment. Jung's notion of conscience arose from his work with analysands in which dreams suggested an innate moral agent that evaluated individual actions and behaviour more deeply than the ego. From the dream of a businessman with dirty hands, Jung hypothesized that there existed an evaluative function within the psyche that was independent of consciousness. He wondered whether there was an unconscious personality who could also comment on our morality and ethics.

For Jung, true and authentic conscience rises above the moral code,[37] which he has defined as a collective "Ten Commandments," a common stock of thoughts and beliefs. The true voice of conscience possesses an authority higher than traditional collective morality or, in Freud's terminology, the superego. This voice of conscience is the individual's expression of psychic truth. "Ordinary morality," Jung suggests, "is a basic law of the unconscious or at any rate influences it. The conclusion stands in flagrant contradiction to the common experience of the autonomy of the unconscious. Although morality as such is a universal attribute of the human psyche, the same cannot be maintained of a given moral code."[38]

At first glance, individual ethical reaction and collective moral code appear to be identical. And this is true as long as there is no conflict—when there is no disagreement between the collective ethics and individual morality. However, the distinction between these two "becomes obvious," Jung writes, "the moment a conflict of duty makes clear the difference between conscience and the moral code. It will then be decided which is the stronger: tradition and conventional morality or conscience."[39] Jungian analyst and long-time colleague of Jung, Marie-Louise von Franz, describes it this way: "If the phenomenon arises within oneself, one generally has a strange feeling of certainty

---

36   Jung, "A Psychological View of Conscience," paragraph 825.
37   *Ibid.*, paragraph 838.
38   *Ibid.*, paragraph 825.
39   *Ibid.*, paragraph 837.

as to what is the right thing to do no matter what the collective code may say about it."[40]

In this context, it is possible to understand Jung's definition of neurosis as being inherently a moral conflict. The psychological symptoms of neurosis reveal a particular, one-sided attitude of the individual, and this indicates a failure of the natural self-regulatory function of the psyche. But Jung's view of neurotic symptoms goes beyond the simple idea that they are an expression of personal psychopathology. He saw them as having a teleological—that is, forward looking—function, and as constituting "conflicts of conscience and difficult moral problems that require an answer."[41] In other words, the individual deviates from the natural laws of her own personality—that is, from her own experience of subjective truth and the natural maturation demanded by the psyche. Real moral problems stem from these conflicts of duty between the outer moral code (Freud's superego) and one's own inner path. The solution, or a synthesizing "third," must come from deep within the personality. For the ethically-minded person, this is the only solution, because the collective moral code cannot be relied upon to help her resolve the dilemma. It is this collision of opposites that can produce psychological illness and even madness as the individual wrestles with her inability to deal with a "problem which is not recognized as such by the world in which she lives."[42] She must suffer through "a living process of personal destiny."[43] This kind of neurosis seems to reflect a disturbance between a collective that has lost its values and the religious function of the psyche through which the activity of the Self is revealed.

It is interesting that Jung returned to an early Judeo-Christian idea when he equated conscience with the *vox Dei*, the "Voice of God." He departed from the Judeo-Christian concept, however, in that conscience, to him, was an inner psychological principle, and notions of God reflected the divine centre in the psyche also known as the Self—the archetype at the root of the ego that reflects the totality of the psyche. "Conscience," Jung wrote, "commands the individual to obey his inner voice even at the risk of going astray."[44]

The psyche is a complicated entity filled with competing complexes, archetypes, desires, and instincts. Given the mercurial dynamic of the uncon-

---

40   Marie-Louise von Franz, *Shadow and Evil in Fairy Tales* (Boston: Shambhala Publications Inc., 1995), p. 140.

41   Jung, "Foreword to Neumann," paragraph 1408.

42   Erich Neumann, *Depth Psychology and the New Ethic* (New York: Harper Torchbooks, 1969), p. 30.

43   *Ibid.*, p. 32.

44   Jung, "A Psychological View of Conscience," paragraph 841.

scious, the conscience, or "Voice of God," is extremely difficult to differentiate from all the other messages that are sent. Archetypes contain light and dark, positive and negative poles—and the unconscious is inherently amoral (without morality) and duplicitous. Therefore, Jung writes, it is not possible to "attribute to the unconscious, a function which appears moral to us."[45] The moral quality of the unconscious depends on consciousness and stands in compensatory relation to it.[46]

❧

Therefore, for Jung, the treatment of certain neuroses was a moral problem rather than a technical one. Conscience, with its connection to the Self, seems to connect to a curative factor that Jung saw as restoring and maintaining psychic balance, and which also moves the personality toward wholeness. This psychic wholeness is connected to our inner morality and to the deeper call of individuation.

---

45 *Ibid.*, paragraph 835.
46 Murray Stein, "Introduction" in *Jung on Evil* (London: Routledge, 1995), p. 6.

CHAPTER 3

Moral Development and Psychopathology

Where there is a lack of moral sense, the implanted moral code is necessary, but the resultant socialization is unstable.[1]

—Donald Winnicott

The debate over the psychic origins of morality discussed in the last two chapters has highlighted the evolutionary and theological perspectives. Jung combined these two perspectives, arriving at the psychological experience of the archetype and the "Voice of God," and identifying the notion of the ego-self axis, that is, the connection between the ego and the personality's inner guiding force. As we have seen, consciousness plays a major role in the making of moral or ethical judgments. Later, we will look at Jung's notion of ego responsibility in relationship to the messages of the unconscious, but first we will concentrate on the roles of consciousness and the ego. In order to do that, we will need to examine some theories of moral development and their descriptions of how the ego develops its ethical stance. Where does our ethical and moral capacity come from? This raises the perennial question of "nature" versus "nurture."

Most developmental psychologists agree that character is developed through the interaction between nature and nurture, that is, an individual's morality arises from the interaction between their inborn disposition and their experience with caregivers and other elements of their early environment. Infants do not come into the world with an innate understanding of right and wrong in terms of collective morality, so moral reasoning or judgement must also be cultivated by caregivers. Leading-edge research into the link between the development of higher human functions and the brain's circuitry shows

---

1   Donald Winnicott, *Maturational Processes and The Facilitating Environment* (London: Karnac Books, 1990).

that there is a strong correlation between this development and the infant's relationship with early caregivers. However, these researchers have also theorized that infants are active participants in the development of their own higher functions, including ethical functions. This suggests that ethical capacity or moral development is affected not only by environmental factors but is also in part innate—derived from the earliest, instinctually driven exchanges with the primary caregiver.[2]

Strong evidence also exists to suggest that children have an innate ethical capability or moral sense that exists apart from prescribed rules. According to studies carried out by University of Chicago's Richard Shweder, children possess an intuitive morality that leads them to spontaneously evaluate the actions and motives of others as worthy or unworthy. These studies involved asking children whether or not it was right to do something—even if there was no explicit rule against it. Children made a distinction between actions and behaviour that were always wrong, such lying and cheating, etc., and actions and behaviour that were wrong because there was a rule prohibiting them. These studies are particularly interesting, as children differentiated between actions that constituted a betrayal of a relationship and actions forbidden by a specific rule. This is distinction highlighted the difference between morality based on relationship (i.e. , Eros) and morality based on rules (i.e., Logos).

In his book, *A Moral Sense*, James Q. Wilson argues that some aspects of morality are universal because of the basic human instinct that seeks affiliation and attachment.[3] His conclusion is based on research into the moralities of other cultures, where he found common moral obligations that cut across many different societies. These obligations focused on conflicts in everyday intimate life—that is, in areas that might be considered in the realm of Eros, relatedness, attachment, and relationship. Contemporary developmental psychologists who have examined infants' instinctual interactions with their mothers have substantiated these findings. The resulting morality is what Murray Stein calls "lunar conscience"—the conscience that rests in the mother, in the instincts, and in Nature. Sympathy and compassion for others are human characteristics and, specifically, we are biologically programmed to care for our children. Wilson goes on to say that violations of a basic sense of affiliation and attachment (that is, relationship) are considered immoral by almost all cultures.

---

2   Hester McFarland Solomon, "The Ethical Attitude in Analytic Training and Practice" (paper presented to the Ethics Matters Conference, Cambridge, July 2003), p. 5.

3   James Q. Wilson, *A Moral Sense* (New York: The Free Press, 1993), p. 127.

Theories of moral development fall broadly into two categories: those based on principles of Logos and those based on principles of Eros. The distinction between the two types was first highlighted in the 1970s by American psychologist Carol Gilligan when she criticized the work of early theorists such as Jean Piaget and Lawrence Kohlberg, claiming that they showed a noticeable bias toward a masculine, or Logos, orientation to this issue. Gilligan was justified in her comments in that traditional theories of moral development tend to be based on principles of reason, judgement, discrimination, principles, rules, and insight. These theories emphasize Logos, objectivity, the principles of the outer world, and the thinking function. Piaget and Kohlberg, for instance, argued that moral development correlates with the development of rational ego processes and is based on cognitive rationality. Hence, moral development and reasoning may not appear until later in childhood or early adolescence. Gilligan's work focused on morality displayed by women, which tends to be contextually based and is associated with Eros, relatedness, responsibility, feeling, and relationship. Moral development then becomes a measure for responsibility and the capacity for relationship—elements associated with the feminine. In her book, *A Different Voice*, Gilligan postulates that there is a distinction between a formal and abstract morality of rights (Logos) and a morality of responsibility (Eros). According to a morality of responsibility, moral dilemmas must be resolved through a contextual and narrative mode of thinking. As she writes: "The concept of morality as concerned with the activity of care centres moral development around the understanding of responsibility and relationships just as a conception of morality as fairness ties moral development to the understanding of rights and rules."[4]

This chapter looks at various theories of moral development—a discussion based on my central premise that individuation is an ethical process with values centred in the Heart. It is the Heart that carries the morality of both Logos and Eros and rests in *Tao* and the Self. This analysis will lay the groundwork for discussions in Part II, which concentrate on the issues of ethics in analysis and boundary violations in psychotherapy and analysis. As we go on to compare moral development theories in this chapter, we will discover how they relate to Logos and Eros. Then we will examine the theories of two prominent psychologists and thinkers on this subject, Erik Erikson and Erich Neumann. Erikson postulates that a morality based on rules and threats is characteristic of childhood morality, whereas the more developed ethical orientation of adulthood recognizes *mutuality*, responsibility, and relationship (based on

---

4   Carol Gilligan, *In a Different Voice* (Cambridge, MA: Harvard University, 1982), p. 19.

Erikson's reformulated Golden Rule). Erich Neumann, on the other hand, equates the development of an ethical orientation with the development of consciousness. We will examine this view before ending the chapter with a discussion of moral psychopathology.

Jean Piaget and Lawrence Kohlberg

The study of moral development in children was pioneered by Swiss psychologist Jean Piaget and later developed by American psychologist Lawrence Kohlberg. Piaget was particularly interested in how children acquired and understood rules for playing games. He felt that "rules" of games could be seen as analogous to the "rules" of society. From his research, Piaget saw that there were three levels of awareness of rules. Children up to four or five years of age do not understand the rules. Piaget defined this as the pre-moral stage of development. In the "moral realism" stage of development—lasting from five to about ten years of age—the rules are understood, but they are seen as coming from a higher authority and therefore unchangeable. In the final stage—from age ten and on—the rules of the game are the product of discussion and dialogue among players and can therefore be changed if everyone agrees. This stage was defined as "moral subjectivism." As children develop new conceptions of the rules, there is a corresponding change in their attitudes toward adults. Beginning with a stance of unilateral respect and obedience, they evolve toward a relationship based on equality with peers. This stage also corresponds to a time period when the child becomes more independent from parents. Piaget observed that boys are more interested in the rules of the game, while girls are more concerned about relationships. This important distinction will be discussed later, in relation to the work of Carol Gilligan.

Lawrence Kohlberg developed his influential theories of moral reasoning by presenting moral dilemmas to a group of American males between the ages of ten and twenty-six. In his studies, he found a correlation between an individual's level of moral reasoning and their level of cognitive development. His theory of moral development involves the process of redefining one's concept of Self "in its relationship to the concept of other people."[5] From this research, he theorized that individuals move through three subdivided levels of moral judgement as they grow up: pre-conventional morality, conventional morality, and post-conventional morality. The highest stages of moral development are

---

5   Stephen Freeman, *Ethics: An Introduction to Philosophy and Practice* (Belmont, CA: Wadsworth Thomson Learning, 2000), p. 102.

characterized by a greater differentiation and understanding of human rights and an increasing ability to arrive at an objectively fair or just resolution of moral dilemmas. In this way, his theories are closely related to the ideas of Immanuel Kant, for whom "moral obligation had to rest on pure reason and in particular on the degree to which the maxim of one's actions could be made a universal principle."[6]

Pre-conventional Morality (Stages 1 and 2): Kohlberg found that this type of morality was exhibited in most children under the age of nine, in many adolescents, and in most adult criminal offenders. Individuals at this level do not fully understand or uphold societal rules and expectations. In Stage 1—Heteronomous Morality, their moral reasoning is based on the avoidance of negative consequences (that is, if you break the rules, you will likely be punished). Kohlberg observed that when there is a greater degree of differentiation, individuals acknowledge that the rules of society are good in cases where following them is in someone's immediate interest. Even at this stage (Stage 2—Individualism), with its greater consideration of equal exchange and agreement, the predominant concern remains for oneself and for survival.

Conventional Morality (Stages 3 and 4): Kohlberg observed that this is the level reached by most adolescents and adults. Individuals conform to what is morally right as defined by the rules, expectations, and conventions of society. Being good means having good motives, showing concern for others, and exhibiting the characteristics of trust, loyalty, respect, and gratitude. (This makes up Stage 3—Mutual Interpersonal Relationships and Expectations). With a greater degree of differentiation, morality evolves to consist of people fulfilling actual duties which they have agreed to undertake, and being morally right involves contributing to society, the group, or institutions. (This is Stage 4—Social System and Conscience.)

Post-conventional Morality (Stages 5 and 6): According to Kohlberg's conceptions, individuals at the post-conventional level understand and accept the rules of society because they understand and accept the moral principles underlying those rules. They are aware that people hold a variety of values and opinions, and that most values and opinions should be upheld in the interests of impartiality because they are part of the social contract between individuals. (This is Stage 5—Social Contract or Utility and Individual Rights.) Where there is a conflict between moral principles and convention, the individual will judge by principle rather than by convention. The highest level of moral development (Stage 6—Universal Ethical Principles) is described as hypothetical

---

6   Wilson, *The Moral Sense*, p. 192.

and based on universal ethical principles such as justice, equality of human rights, and respect for the dignity of human beings as individual persons.

Carol Gilligan and Gender Differences

Carol Gilligan, Associate Professor of Education at Harvard University, argues in her book, *In A Different Voice*, that traditional developmental theorists have implicitly adopted a masculine model of development and that women's experiences and perceptions reveal a different model. Women tend to be overly sensitive to the needs of others and this "moral weakness," as advanced by Freud and Piaget, is actually women's moral strength. "Women's moral weakness," she writes,

> manifests in an apparent diffusion and confusion of judgement, and is thus inseparable from women's moral strength, an overriding concern with relationship and responsibilities. The reluctance to judge may itself be indicative of the care and concern for others that infuse the psychology of women's development and are responsible for what is generally seen as problematic in its nature.[7]

The knowledge of intimacy, relationship, and care has been considered intuitive and instinctive, and Gilligan believes that women's moral development centres on the elaboration of that knowledge. The result is a morality of responsibility that emphasizes connection, relatedness, and Eros, and acknowledges the complexity and multifaceted character of real people and real situations. Ethical conflicts arise from conflicting responsibilities related to the consideration of the individual, how to be responsible in the world, and how to lead a moral life (which includes obligations to oneself and to others). The problem becomes one of limiting responsibilities without abandoning moral concern.

Using Kohlberg's broad three-level framework, Gilligan conducted a study of women who faced an abortion decision. Her hypothesis was that morality based on the feminine principles of Eros and an "Ethic of Care" becomes progressively more developed with a greater understanding of human relationship. As a result, there is an increasing differentiation between self and the Other, and a growing comprehension of the dynamics of social interaction.

---

7   Gilligan, *In a Different Voice*, pp. 16–17.

Level One: The initial focus of women at this level (which would corre-spond to Kohlberg's Pre-conventional Morality) is on caring for oneself in order to ensure survival. Concerns are very pragmatic at first, but this stance is then assessed in light of sanctions imposed by society. At some point, women experience this attitude as selfish and move on to a transition phase, where others are viewed as more important.

Level Two: At this level, women consider that they cannot be moral and good without caring for others—a position often taken to the exclusion of one's own self-interest. In the transition from Level One to Level Two, the issue is one of attachment and connection to others. Conceptions of what is selfish and what is responsible also make their first appearance at this stage of moral reasoning. As the individual tends to others and moves toward social partici-pation, their sense of self-worth is enhanced. Morality and moral judgement are based on shared norms and expectations, and dependence on acceptance by others. Decisions tend to entail a sacrifice of someone's needs in deference to the Other. Clearly, the conventional feminine voice, which corresponds to Kohlberg's Conventional Morality, is based on societal conceptions of good-ness and self-worth rooted in the ability to care for and protect others.

Level Three: The focus at this level is on the dynamics of relationships. Because of a greater understanding of the interconnection between self and the Other, there is a dissipation of the tension that women experienced at Level Two as they moved from selfishness to responsibility. The Ethic of Care now becomes a self-chosen principle of judgement, and becomes universal in its condemnation of exploitation and hurt. The transition between Levels Two and Three becomes a shift in concern from goodness to truth. Women reconsider their relationship between self and Other, and scrutinize the logic of self-sacrifice in the service of morality or care. As individuals re-exam-ine responsibility, they integrate what other people think with a new inner judgement that is able to differentiate between the voice of self and the voice of others, one which demands honesty and taking responsibility for oneself. The morality of an action is assessed in terms of the realities of its intention, its consequences, and the willingness to accept responsibility for choice.

Erik Erikson's Ethical Orientation

Erik Erikson, a German-born psychologist, was a Freudian and an ego–psychologist. A large part of his work explored the relationship between the individual and society, and the psychological development of the individual over a lifetime. His theory of an ethical orientation in adulthood suggests that conscience and the development of a mature ethical attitude are part of normal psychological development. He identified eight stages of development, beginning in infancy and extending to old age (depicted in Table 1, below). During each stage of the life cycle, an individual has a development task and must negotiate through a psychosocial crisis of opposites. The successful negotiation of each stage results in the development of psychosocial virtues, where the ego learns to identify the appropriate positive-negative balance of each pole. Another word for virtue, according to Erikson, might be ego strength.

It is important to emphasize this notion of ego strength, as it is an indication of the coherence of the ego complex. The ego is the centre of consciousness in the personality, and it is the carrier of subjective personality. It must make its ethical decisions, as well as evaluating the messages of the unconscious. Erikson would also suggest that "ego strength means the ability to maintain the wholeness of the personality"[8]—that is, the ego must maintain its integrity in the face of the various challenges it encounters.

---

8   Quoted in John Beebe, *Integrity in Depth* (New York: Fromm International Publishing, 1995), p. 126.

Erik Erikson's Eight Stages of Psychosocial Development

Stage and Age	Psychosocial Crisis	Significant Relations	Psychosocial Modalities	Psychosocial Virtues
Stage I Infant *(ages 0–1)*	trust vs. mistrust	mother	to get, to give in return	hope, faith
Stage II Toddler *(ages 2–3)*	autonomy vs. shame and doubt	parents	to hold on, to let go	will, determination
Stage III Pre-schooler *(ages 3–6)*	initiative vs. guilt	family	to go after, to play	purpose, courage
Stage IV School-age child *(ages 7–12 or so)*	industry vs. inferiority	neighbourhood and school	to complete, to make things together	competence
Stage V Adolescence *(ages 12–18 or so)*	ego-identity vs. role confusion	peer groups, role models	to be oneself, to share oneself	fidelity, loyalty
Stage VI Young adult *(late teens to early twenties)*	intimacy vs. isolation	partners, friends	to lose and find oneself in another	love
Stage VII Middle adult *(late twenties to fifties)*	generativity vs. self-absorption	household, workmates	to make, to be taken care of	care
Stage VIII Old adult *(fifties and beyond)*	integrity vs. despair	mankind or "my kind"	to be, through having been, to face not being	wisdom

Erikson's theory of moral development exists in tandem with his theory of psychosocial development, and his contribution to this discussion is a developmental theory of conscience and ethical values throughout the life cycle. The other theories discussed thus far imply that our ethical capacity is fully formed by late adolescence. Erikson suggests that the maturation of our ethical capacity undergoes development well into adulthood and, as a result, we are continually working on our ethical discrimination. His concept of a mature ethical orientation is a significant contribution in light of current ethical paradigms of moral relativism based on tolerance and cultural relativity.

Erikson makes a clear distinction between the moral orientation of children and the ethical sense of adults. He saw the first as the internalization of social prohibition, which we identified as Freud's superego. The latter reflects the development of an ethical orientation that is based on a mature, adult, ethical perspective. This is how he saw the distinction:

> ... ethical orientation ... really marks the difference between adulthood and adolescence—"ethical" meaning a universal sense of values assented to with insight and foresight, in anticipation of immediate responsibilities, not the least of which is a transmission of these values to the next generation.[9]

> I would consider ethical rules to be based on ideals to be striven for with a high degree of rational assent and with a ready consent to a formulated good, a definition of perfections, and some promise of self-realization.[10]

According to Erikson's theory, the beginnings of conscience and ethical development come at the third stage of development of early childhood, ages two to six. This stage also marks the beginning of the child's collective moral orientation and the development of the superego. During this phase, the child experiences the psychosocial crisis of initiative versus guilt. The child is physically able to move around and experiences the ability to take initiative in her environment. However, this increasing sense of independence is accompanied by guilt as the child meets with opposition from society and from others in her environment. This period of development also corresponds to Freud's Oedi-

---

9   Walter Conn, "Erik Erikson: Ethical Orientation, Conscience and the Golden Rule," *Journal of Religious Ethics* 5.2 (Fall 1977), p. 251.

10   Erik Erikson, *Insight and Responsibility: Lectures on the Ethical Implications of Psychoanalytic Insight* (New York: W.W. Norton, 1964), p. 222.

pus complex and to the child's sexual awakening and discovery. Guilt becomes a key experience as limitations imposed from outside teach the child to control impulses and restrain her from acting on her fantasies. The development of conscience during Stage III consists of an inner voice of self-observation. Internalized, it represents the beginning of Freud's superego and can become a source of self-doubt and punishment. Developmentally, this is Erikson's first ethical principle: moral rules, which are enforced by threats or punishment. The child behaves in an "acceptable way" because of fear of abandonment, public exposure, shame, or isolation. It is not the rule itself that affects behaviour but the threat.

Erikson's second ethical proposition or principle—Ideology and Ideals—corresponds to the fifth stage of development, which occurs during adolescence. This is the time for an adolescent to experiment with ideology as he looks for answers to the question "Who am I?" At this point, the individual stands between childhood and adulthood, and experiences a process of developing the beliefs, values, and attitudes that will make up his philosophy of life. This stage also represents the middle point between the morality of childhood and a set of more mature adult ethics. Erikson defined ideology as "a system of commanding ideas held together more (but not exclusively) by totalistic logic and utopian conviction than by cognitive understanding or pragmatic experience."[11] This search involves a meaningful set of values that contributes to the adolescent's worldview—the philosophy that will serve him as he makes his way into the world. If this stage is mastered successfully, the individual will acquire a progressive, tolerant, and diverse ideology, which Erikson sees as critical to making the transition to a higher form of ethics. If this stage is not mastered, the individual's ideology can become rigid, arrogant, fixed, and exclusive. Therefore, the person is not open to the real subjectivity of the Other, and in this exclusivity, all the unacceptable parts become relegated to the Shadow and are disowned.

For Erikson, like Jung, responsibility is synonymous with a mature adult ethical sense. He believes that responsibility consists of more than just following rules and behaviour, morals, and laws. His concept of an ethical orientation involves values, beliefs, and a philosophy of life—that is, the ideology developed by the individual in adolescence. But this step is only one along a developmental path that eventually leads to responsibility. For Erikson,

---

11   J. Eugene Wright, *Erikson: Identity and Religion* (New York: The Seabury Press, 1982), p. 119.

responsibility is an ethical norm,[12] and conscience is at a higher level of development than the superego. He saw conscience as the great governor of initiative—"the inner voice of self-observation, self-guidance, and self-punishment. Conscience can have a primitive, infantile component and it is, to whatever extent, never completely separated from the superego. Walter Conn, however, suggests that the distinction Erikson makes regarding conscience

> opens up the possibility of understanding conscience not as the mere internalization of social prohibitions, but as an active striving for ideals …. By identifying conscience with a mature ethical orientation, Erikson helps us to understand that a full human conscience is not part of a man's birthright, but an achievement of normative human development.[13]

Erikson's third, fourth, and fifth ethical propositions relate to adult development, which he saw as beginning in Stage VI, the "young adult" phase centred on "intimacy vs. isolation." (Unlike the stages in childhood, it is not so easy to differentiate stages through adulthood.) The third ethical proposal is "emerging responsibility"—the beginning of a "true ethical sense,"[14] which rests in mutuality. The young adult becomes concerned about relationships and intimacy, and recognizes the difference between self and the Other. It is essential that the identity stage be successfully mastered, otherwise love and intimacy degenerate into fusion and loss of identity. Mutuality and responsibility are intimately linked in Erikson's thinking regarding ethics. The origins of the psychological experience of mutuality lie in Stage I and grow out of the development of trust through the earliest interactions with the mother. Mutuality is a function of Eros and entails reciprocity and intimacy, and Eros, "our united feeling-link with other people,"[15] embodies Martin Buber's concept of the "I-Thou" relationship. In fact, Buber used the word mutuality to reflect an "I-Thou" relationship—one that is reciprocal, open, caring, loving, and respectful and characterized by dialogue. It stands in contrast to an "I-It" attitude toward relationship, where the Other is seen only as an object without independent feelings or opinions, to be used for one's own purposes. Mutuality therefore reflects the ability of one person to relate to another in the Other's

---

12   *Ibid.*, p. 102.
13   Conn, *Erik Erikson*, p. 255.
14   Wright, *Erikson*, p. 121.
15   Mario Jacoby, *The Analytical Encounter: Transference and Human Relationship* (Toronto: Inner City Books, 1984), p. 64.

totality and genuine otherness. Mario Jacoby suggests that "to relate to the otherness of Thou, I have to know who I am."[16] It is therefore not surprising that Erikson sees the true development of mutuality as coming after the identity crisis of adolescence. It is not until adulthood that mutuality is fully developed and integrated, but the first experience of it appears in the relationship between the infant and the mother or other primary caregiver. This relationship becomes the foundation for all relationships later in life.

The notions of mutuality and responsibility are further developed in Erikson's fourth ethical proposition. It is here that the idea of generativity becomes important. As noted above, Erikson's ethical theory involves passing on ethical values to the next generation. He sees its development in adulthood as belonging to Stage VII—the generativity vs. self-absorption phase.

The final ethical proposition is "Active Choice—Responsibility choosing the ethical sense." Erikson defined active choice as "an active and giving attitude rather than a demanding or dependent one."[17] It implies consciousness and an ego choice to live one's life in accordance with one's ethical values and orientation. This idea is very close to Jung's ethical challenge of individuation.

Erikson's ethical theory is synthesized in his reformulation of the Golden Rule in light of his theory of psychosocial development. The Golden Rule essentially says, "Do unto others as you would have them do unto you." It reflects an ethic of reciprocity that is found in the writings of every religious tradition. In the Christian religion, we know it from the Gospels of Matthew, Mark, and Luke: "All things whatsoever ye would that men should do to you, do ye even so to them: for this is the law and the prophets." (Matthew 7:12) In the East, Confucius and Mencius articulated the ethic this way: "Try your best to treat others as you would wish to be treated yourself, and you will find that this is the shortest way to benevolence." (Mencius VII.A.4.) Erikson's ethical propositions of generativity, mutuality, and active choice also reflect this philosophy: "Truly worthwhile acts enhance a mutuality between the doer and the other—a mutuality which strengthens the doer even as it strengthens the other. Thus the 'doer' and 'the other' are partners in one deed."[18]

Erikson's concept of ethics involves the active participation of the ego in its maturation through life. However, he did not forget the ability of the unconscious to challenge ethical capacity and attitudes. He writes:

---

16   *Ibid.*, p. 63.
17   Wright, *Erikson*, p. 126.
18   Erik Erikson, *Insight and Responsibility. Lectures on the Ethical Implications of Psychoanalytic Insight* (New York: Norton, 1964), p. 223.

While the Golden Rule in its classical versions prods man to strive consciously for a highest good and to avoid mutual harm with a sharpened awareness, our insights assume an unconscious substratum of ethical strength and, at the same time, unconscious arsenals of destructive rage. The last century has traumatically expanded man's awareness of unconscious motivations stemming from his animal ancestry, from his economic history, and from his inner estrangements. It has also created (in all these respects) methods of productive self-analysis. These I consider the pragmatic Western version of that universal trend toward self-scrutiny which once reached such heights in Asian tradition.[19]

Neumann's Ethical Development of Consciousness

In his book *Depth Psychology and a New Ethic*,[20] Erich Neumann suggests that the evolution of ethics is closely linked with the evolution of consciousness both for the individual and for the group to which she belongs. Like Erikson, Neumann saw a correlation between increased ethical awareness and the emergence of the ego from the primary unity of the unconscious: as the ego gains strength and coherence and separates itself from the unconscious or the group, ethical awareness is further differentiated. (Neumann's exploration of the cultural development of ethics gives psychological support to the work of present-day social biologists such as Edward O. Wilson.) His hypothesis is that the individual's ethical development is intimately tied to the evolution of society.

Neumann identifies two stages in the ethical development of a society or group, along with an interim stage separating the two. He defines Stage One as the primal stage. At this point, the ego is in a state of primary unity with the unconscious—that is, there is no individual consciousness. The individual lives in a state of *participation mystique* with the tribe in which he lives, dominated by the collective psyche. There is no individual or conscious ethical responsibility because the individual remains at the level of the group. In such situations, mob psychologies are likely to result. Since the individual abdicates his ethical responsibility to the group, that entire group or family bears the consequences of the immoral acts of individual members.

The leader of the group expresses ethical values. Such a leader carries the projection of the Self and becomes the creative centre for the group, giving it

---

19 Erikson, *Insight and Responsibility*, p. 243.
20 Erich Neumann, *Depth Psychology and The New Ethic*.(New York: Harper Torchbooks, 1969).

its values and moral leadership. The "Voice of God," reflecting ethical values, is then revealed to the leader or a few chosen individuals who transmit these values to the group. One example of a leader like this is Moses, who brought the Ten Commandments down to the Israelites after God revealed them to him. This pattern can be found among other leaders of great religions, including Jesus, Buddha, and Confucius. Through the transmission from the founder to the disciples, one individual's religious and ethical values are transformed into a collective ethical code. As Neumann writes:

> We can trace this source of the collective ethic in revelations to Founder Individuals throughout human history from primitive man right down to civilized nations. The utterances of gods, the decisions of seers and medicine-men, priests, chiefs and the divinely possessed from oracles and judgements delivered by a god to the revelation of the deity in a god-given law—all these are unique acts of revelation born out of a particular situation. At a later date, they are collected and codified and endowed with an abstract and universal validity.[21]

Neumann identified an interim stage where the primary unity that had characterized the beginning of ego development disintegrates. Individual consciousness emerges and separates from the tribe, but it is then subject to collective law. This is an important step in the development of consciousness, where the ego differentiates and strengthens itself as it separates from the unconscious. The collective values, which are now law, carry the good and the light. Both the individual and the group begin to develop a sense of identity and create ideals to aspire to. And when the unconscious erupts in an *enantiodromia*[22]—that is, when the opposite of the collective ideals manifest themselves, the tribe or collective believes these unknown forces are the "powers of darkness" and "declares war" on them in order to protect the status quo of the current collective ethic. Evil and the Shadow are projected outwardly and experienced objectively. This stage of development, Neumann suggests, is a stage of repression and suppression of the unconscious. He has used the term "old ethic" to describe this stage and suggests that it reflects the current moral ethic of the Western world. He also indicates that it may have been a neces-

---

21   *Ibid.*, p. 62.

22   A psychological law first outlined by Heraclitus, which says that sooner or later, everything turns into its opposite. Jung saw this as a psychic law of development that was equally relevant for individuals and for collectives.

sary stage in the evolutionary development of ego consciousness because it is through the suppression of the emotionality of the unconscious that human beings were liberated from the primary unity with it.

The second ethical stage is the stage of individual moral responsibility. It occurs as individual ego consciousness continues a process of differentiation out of the tribe or collective but remains within the framework of collective values. The individual, aware of the collective moral code, exercises his personal responsibility by trying to put those values into practice. For the individual who must now accept moral responsibility, the experience of the instinctual forces and energies of the unconscious, which take possession of the ego, are considered sinful. Because there is consciousness, the ego experiences an intra-psychic conflict when it has been possessed by the unconscious. It is no longer in a state of undifferentiated ignorance and so has some consciousness about what it is experiencing. Metaphorically, the individual has eaten of the Tree of the Knowledge of Good and Evil and has been cast out of the Garden of Eden. Individual responsibility involves a relationship to conscience and to the ideal that has been established by the leaders of the community. Psychologically, it can result in a splitting of the personality: a *persona* is formed, which identifies with the false self or facade while all personality characteristics that do not conform to collective values are pushed into the Shadow.

Moral Psychopathology

Thus far, I have explored natural and healthy moral development through the work of several noted theorists. When this development goes awry because of early childhood wounding or other forms of psychopathology, moral pathology is the consequence. There seem to be two main types of moral pathology: a denial of conscience, which might be found in a narcissistic personality disorder, and the complete lack of conscience that might be found in psychopathic personalities. Both disorders reflect injuries to the individual's ability to relate to the Other and or to act upon Erikson's notion of mutuality. What defines these disorders as pathology is not the specific behaviour itself but the individual's relationship to the behaviour. The relationship to the behaviour reveals the degree to which the psychic function of conscience is at work and the degree to which it is diseased.

The DSM[23] includes in its definition of narcissism "lack of empathy"

---

23   American Psychiatric Association, *Diagnostic and Statistical Manual of Mental Disorders*, 4th ed. (Washington, DC: American Psychiatric Association, 2000).

and "the demonstrated inability to recognize the subjective experiences and feelings of others." Narcissistic individuals are unable to hear the Other—an interaction that is essential to ethical discourse— because they are unwilling to suffer through the painful experience of self-examination or to submit themselves to the demands of their conscience. In such cases, individuals are more than able to sacrifice others in order to protect their ego ideal. Those who have this disorder are unable to tolerate the psychological ambivalence that is created when conscience is constellated. Rather than suffer the pain of self-examination, they project it onto others through scapegoating in order to preserve their self-image. It is as if they are unable to acknowledge the Shadow, sin, or their own imperfection. In this kind of pathology, a great deal of energy is directed to projection, denial, and rationalization, and the individual is unable to give himself over to a higher will.

The other kind of moral pathology—psychopathology—is characterized as a complete lack of conscience. It is as if the psychic function of conscience is non-existent. Marie-Louise von Franz describes it in this way: "in psychopathic patients, we often meet a seemingly complete heartlessness, no feeling and no ethics. Behind this is a hidden secret inflation, for they behave as if they had the right to lie, cheat, and murder with no self-doubt and no self-criticism."[24]

In his book *The Emptied Soul*,[25] Adolf Guggenbühl-Craig identifies several symptoms that are typical of this disorder. He suggests that such individuals are unable to love, have a deficient sense of morality, lack psychic development, and have no real understanding of or insight into themselves. They demonstrate lack of remorse or guilt over their actions, are manipulative, and are callous. There is a basic failure of Eros or feeling. In its severest form, individuals exhibit very little concern about their behaviour. Often they are very intelligent but demonstrate a noticeable lack of moral sense. For the most part, they tend to live a "predatory" lifestyle, where they see others in terms of how they can be used as stimulation or to build up their self-esteem or material value. In an earlier version of the DSM, this disorder was listed under sociopathic personality. In the DSM IV, it is listed under "anti-social personality disorder" and is described as the "disregard and violation of the rights of others" by means of deceit or manipulation for personal profit, and a lack of remorse at hurting others.

---

24   Marie-Louise von Franz, *Shadow and Evil in Fairy Tales* (Boston: Shambhala, 1974), p. 272.

25   Adolf Guggenbühl-Craig, *The Emptied Soul: On the Nature of the Psychopath* (Woodstock: Spring Publications, 1980).

In Chapter 1, I suggested that morality, conscience, and ethical values set up a dialectic between self-interest and some Other, where the dictates of the Other are superior to ego self-interest. It is, however, the ego that must make the differentiation and the decision in favour of conscience or not. In some cases, the psychic function of the conscience is diseased and unable to function properly. In other cases, the person making the decision is at an early stage of moral development. As we have seen in this chapter, various theories of moral development outline the stages through which a child develops his ethical capacity, the various forms the Other can take, and the developing relationship between the ego and the Other. For Piaget and Kohlberg, the rules of society constitute the Other. Carol Gilligan suggests that feminine moral development rests in relationship and Eros. Erikson argues that responsibility and mutuality are the result of moral development. It is clear from all these theories that moral development does not exist in isolation but is intimately connected to the relationship between the individual and the group or society to which she belongs. At the same time, our ethical capacity and awareness reflect later stages of our development and are linked with our sense of individuality and wholeness. It is this individuality and wholeness that I believe is found in the Heart and in our integrity.

CHAPTER 4

The Heart: The Ethics of Integrity and Authenticity

Look at a man in the midst of doubt and danger, and you will learn in his hour of adversity what he really is. It is then that true utterances are wrung from the recesses of his breast. The mask is torn off; and the reality remains.

—Roman philosopher Lucretius

Speech is not of the tongue but of the heart. The tongue is merely the instrument with which one speaks. He who is dumb is dumb in his heart, not in his tongue ... as you speak, so is your heart.

—Paracelsus

I sat in my analyst's office. I was deeply ashamed of myself. My Shadow—all that I had repressed—was beginning to stink. Just when I expected her to say she thought I was the most reprehensible person she had ever worked with, her response launched something absolutely new in me. She said that what she remembered most about her analysands was the "integrity" of the work. I was fascinated. What did that mean? Where does the psyche's integrity come from?

The word integrity derives from the Latin *integritas*, which means "entire." *Integrate* and *integration* also come from that Latin root, and their meaning relates to the combining of disparate elements into a harmonious entity. Unlike the philosophical discussions of ethics and morality, the notion of integrity is more rooted in psychology. It alludes to an inner psychological harmony or wholeness, as well as to an individual's moral character. It is my proposition that the Heart embodies our wholeness and integrity. Integrity serves to integrate thinking and feeling, or Logos and Eros. It is the centre point where Kohlberg's Ethics of Human Rights and Gilligan's Ethic of Care come together.

This knowledge would appear to be lost to Western religious and spiritual traditions. "Heart knowledge" is no longer detached, differentiated, and transpersonal, but in most Western traditions, has become personal, dependent, syrupy, and sentimental, as if with Western over-rationalization, feeling has been reduced to longing. Nevertheless, a higher form of Heart knowledge resides in the collective unconscious. The ancients knew this very well.

It is also in the Heart that we can explore our spiritual journey or individuation process. In his book, *A Path with Heart*, Jack Kornfield, an American spiritual teacher and former Buddhist monk, suggests that our spiritual journey is linked to our deepest love and connected to the Heart. Undertaking such a journey can transform and touch the centre of our being. The goal of the spiritual journey is not about spirit *per se*, with its connections to enlightenment, bliss, knowledge, and ecstasy. Rather, Kornfield says that the transformation of our life patterns is done in the Heart, through compassion and understanding. He writes:

> To awaken the heart of compassion and wisdom in a response to all circumstances is to become a Buddha. When we awaken the Buddha within ourselves, we awaken the universal force of spirit that can bring compassion and understanding to the whole of the world .... It is the power of our heart that brings wisdom and freedom in any circumstance that brings the kingdom of the spirit alive here on earth.[1]

Integrity and Authenticity

The various definitions of integrity imply a pure and deep virtue, and like the function of conscience in the human psyche, integrity extends beyond ego wishes and desires. Cicero, the Roman statesman and Stoic philosopher who lived during the later years of the Roman Republic, first discussed the idea in *Ex-Officits*. He wrote about integrity as a moral obligation, as a standard of reputation, and as a way of being in the world, which he saw it as a general

---

1   Jack Kornfield, *A Path with Heart* (New York: Bantam Books, 1994), pp. 283–284.

intelligence that guides one to live in accord with Nature's law and one's own nature.

As mentioned previously, the Chinese word for integrity is *te*, and it is central to the teachings of the *Tao Te Ching*. Early texts from the Chou period (1100 to 600 BCE) define *te* as character, intentions, disposition, and personal strength and worth. It is the sum of one's actions, and it reflects the moral weight of an individual. *The Oxford Companion of Philosophy* defines integrity as "the quality of a person who can be counted upon to give precedence to moral considerations even when there is a strong inducement to let self-interest or some clamant desire override them, or when betrayal of moral principle might pass undetected."[2] In the standard dictionary definition, integrity is also the quality or state of being complete, in an unbroken condition, whole, or untouched. It denotes, as well, the quality or state of being of sound moral principle, and it suggests uprightness, honesty, and sincerity. Integrity functions as the glue which binds our character into an integrated whole.

Many moral philosophers have not addressed the concept of integrity directly, likely because it is more a psychological idea than a philosophical one. When we say that a person has integrity, we are recognizing in them some inner psychological harmony and coherence which enables them to take responsibility for their actions. In *The Psychology of Mature Spirituality*, Polly Young-Eisendrath and Melvin Miller suggest that integrity is part of a mature spirituality and reflects an "acceptance of one's limitations, groundedness in the ordinary and the willingness to be surprised."[3] They go on to say that neither the archetypal world of the divine nor the everyday world of humanity can save us from having to confront our character, our fate, or ourselves: "And so we must get used to working with ourselves as we are—with blind spots and imperfections—so that we can become more truthful and compassionate in our development."[4] John Beebe suggests that "the implication is that the real pleasure in exercising integrity in dealings with others is the discovery of integrity itself."[5]

The connection between the meanings of the noun *integrity* and the verb *to integrate* is particularly relevant to Jungian psychology, in which the individ-

---

2   Ted Honderich, ed., *The Oxford Companion to Philosophy* (Oxford: Oxford University Press, 1995).

3   Polly Young-Eisendrath and Melvin Miller, "Introduction" in *The Psychology of Mature Spirituality: Integrity, Wisdom and Transcendence* (London: Routledge, 2000), p. 4.

4   *Ibid.*

5   John Beebe, *Integrity in Depth*, (New York: Fromm International Publishing Corporation, 1995), p. 15.

uation process is often described as one of assimilating the unconscious. This implies recognition or awareness of some previously unknown parts of the personality, an awareness which is then brought into ego consciousness and owned as part of oneself. Diagnostically, the opposite of integration would be disassociation or disintegration.

Integrity promotes wholeness, and wholeness reflects a unity of the outside (i.e., the persona) and the inside (i.e., the ego as the carrier of personality). Integrity is also linked to an individual's ethical capacity and to the development of a mature, ethical attitude toward the Other. This is the position of contemporary moral philosopher Zygmunt Bauman, who notes that "ethical capacity is derived from a system of value and meaning-making that belongs to a different, higher order and unconditional realm of relating to the other. It is the unique and non-reversible nature of my responsibility to another, regardless of whether the other sees their duties in the same way towards me."[6]

One acts out of this wholeness when outside behaviour meets inside authenticity and reveals an inner coherence. Like the dynamic relationship between ethics and morality, the relationship between integrity and authenticity may be defined in this way: Integrity is the ability to distinguish what is genuine and authentic both in oneself and in others, whereas authenticity is the ability to bring that knowledge of action or behaviour into the world. At this point, a psychological synthesis of knowledge, action, and acknowledgement is reached. There is consciousness of what is right and wrong, action is taken on that knowledge of right and wrong even if it means personal cost, and finally there is awareness that one is acting out of one's integrity. This synthesis is not so much about one's duty toward others but about a person's commitments to him- or herself. Failure to honour such commitments reflects a move against the Self and may promote disintegration of the personality.

Authenticity stands for what is genuine, real, and worthy of trust, belief, or acceptance. It is an expression of the degree to which we can assign truth to something. The word derives from the Greek *authentes* and means "one acting on one's own authority." In the German language, the word also has the connotation "to own." In life, being authentic means that you own your life and take responsibility for it, and this bears a striking similarity to the definition of integrity. Being inauthentic suggests an "unowned" life. The German philosopher Heidegger suggests that "authenticity is a matter of choosing to

---

6   Quoted in Hester McFarland Solomon, "The Ethical Attitude in Analytical Training and Practice" (paper presented at IAAP Ethics Matters Conference, Cambridge, England, July 2003), p. 4.

choose, that is, of making one's choices one's own and so being answerable and responsible for one's life."[7]

In his book *The Ethics of Authenticity*, Canadian philosopher Charles Taylor suggests that lack of authenticity is one of the greatest malaises of contemporary society. He observes that the current moral paradigm of self-fulfilment, or being "true to oneself," is rooted in moral relativism.[8] Unlike Jung's concept of the "Voice of God," this position is based on a narcissistic understanding of oneself, egotism, and self-indulgence; it is neither a reflection of the Self nor an authenticity that comes from deep within the personality.

The Enlightenment produced a significant change in thinking about morality in the West. As discussed earlier, the philosophers of this period advocated a type of individualism that emphasized reason and rationality. For these thinkers, personal responsibility did not originate from faith in the Church or in God as the divine presence but rather originated from a faith in personal reason and individual choice. The voice of morality is the voice of individual choice. Charles Taylor believes that "morality has in a sense a voice within,"[9] which is at the foundation of our personality. This stands in opposition to the Christian theological view of an all-powerful and good God. Taylor's ideal of "being true to myself means being true to my own originality, and that is something that only I can articulate and discover. In articulating it, I am also defining myself. I am realizing a potentiality that is properly my own."[10] Taylor's statement highlights a subtle favouring of a morality rooted in integrity and authenticity over a selfish morality. The former is not just about meeting one's own needs—it is about discovering one's uniqueness; it is the process of recognizing one's authentic Self and one's inner life. Jung's definition of conscience as the "Voice of God" is also based on the idea that integrity reflects a person's knowledge of their wholeness and their authenticity. It suggests that our integrity is a struggle for a broader consciousness—something above ego wishes or self-centredness.

Marie-Louise von Franz suggests that one's integrity is the innocent nucleus of the personality or its innermost ethical kernel. This quality is often portrayed in fairy tales by the Simpleton, the Fool, or the Dummling, who

---

7   Quoted in Charles Guignon, "Authenticity and Integrity: A Heideggerian Perspective" in *The Psychology of Mature Spirituality* (London: Routledge, 2000), p. 71.

8   *Moral relativism* is defined in Chapter 1.

9   Charles Taylor, *The Ethics of Authenticity* (Cambridge: Harvard University Press, 1991), p. 26.

10   *Ibid.*, p. 29.

finds the truth through his purity of intention and naïveté. As Von Franz puts it: "he symbolizes the basic genuineness and integrity of the personality. If people do not have in their innermost essence, genuineness, or a certain integrity, they are lost when meeting the problem of evil. They get caught. This integrity is more important than intelligence or self-control or anything else."[11] She goes on to say: "you might say that this inner ethical integrity comes not from the ego but from the Self. It is a genuine reaction which comes from the depth of the personality."[12]

The experience of integrity is a great mystery and von Franz says that this nucleus of integrity is already the secret of an individuated personality. Integrity therefore reflects something of a person's divine spark. A key factor in any analysis, it is what gives the individual the ability to confront the contents of the unconscious. Seen in this way, an inner genuine feeling (i.e., integrity) would be impervious and superior to the irrationality of complexes and all the emotions they bring. Intense emotions stemming from personal need such as fear, desire, hunger, fatigue, anger, or pain arise from complexes that overtake the ego, and they test one's integrity. Integrity gives the individual the courage and fortitude to face those emotions.

Symbolically, analytical psychology has equated the Self with the symbol of the Child. In "The Psychology of the Child Archetype," Jung writes :

> The Child is born out of the womb of the unconscious, begotten out of the depths of human nature or rather out of living Nature herself. It is a personification of vital forces quite outside the limited range of our conscious mind; of ways and possibilities of which our one-sided conscious mind knows nothing; a wholeness that embraces the very depths of Nature. It represents the strongest, the most ineluctable urge in every being, namely the urge to realize itself. It is, as it were, an *incarnation of the inability to do otherwise*, equipped with all the powers of nature and instinct, whereas the conscious mind is always getting caught up in its supposed ability to *do otherwise*. The urge and compulsion to self-realization is a law of nature and thus of invincible power even though its effect, at the start, is insignificant and improbable. Its power is revealed in the miraculous deeds of the child hero ... [13]

---

11   Marie-Louise von Franz, *Shadow and Evil in Fairy Tales* (Boston: Shambhala, 1995), p. 222.

12   *Ibid.*, p. 239.

13   C.G. Jung, "The Psychology of the Child Archetype" in *The Archetypes and the Collective Unconscious*, Vol. 9(i) of *The Collected Works* (Princeton, NJ: Princeton University Press, 1969), paragraph 289.

The archetype of the Child embodies innocent wisdom and vulnerability, as well as a drive toward individuation. Nevertheless, there is a paradox in the symbol of the Child because it also contains aspects of our personality that are undifferentiated. It is as if our intuitive morality and integrity are also symbolically reflected in the childlike parts of our self. Researchers who have studied the morality of children have advanced this hypothesis. According to Richard Sweder from the University of Chicago, "the child is an intuitive moralist,"[14] and he suggests that children recognize moral issues early in their lives.

So what is the source with which we must connect in order to find our authenticity and our integrity? I believe that it is the Heart.

The Symbol of the Heart

Physiologically, the Heart is the centre of biological life. Without it, physical, incarnated life cannot be sustained. Centrally located in the body, it sends blood throughout, pumping with great force and pressure and providing each cell with oxygen and food. Even early humans saw the connection between the heart and life: the Heart was identified with the soul, was seen as the centre of intellect, emotion, religious experience, courage, and strength, and took on a symbolic meaning in spiritual and mystical meditations. For some ancient cultures and mythologies, it was involved in ritualistic sacrifices. For example, in the Aztec and Mayan cultures, ritual human sacrifices were performed that included removing the beating heart as an offering to the gods. It was believed that these sacrifices were needed to keep the sun moving in the sky. Other ancient societies believed that if you ate the heart of the enemy, his strength would become your own.

In the Judeo-Christian tradition, the Heart was thought to be the inner personality that reflected spiritual truth. For the Hebrews and ancient Semites, it was the locus of moral and religious life. Several passages in the Old Testament point to the Heart as an organ of sight, which perceives and therefore understands the divine. This passage from the Book of Jeremiah is one example: "'I shall put my word within them and write it on their hearts,' says Yahveh" (Jeremiah 31:33).[15] And in Ephesians1:18, the apostle Paul tells the Ephesians he is praying for them, so "that the eyes of your heart may be enlightened in order that you may know the hope to which he has called you."

---

14   Richard Shweder, Elliot Turiel, and N.C. Much, "The Moral Intuitions of the Child," in *Social Cognitive Development* (New York: Cambridge University Press, 1981).

15   Mircea Eliade, *The Enclopaedia of Religion* (New York: MacMillan Publishing, 1987), p. 235.

Beginning possibly with St. Augustine, the Heart in the Christian tradition evolved into a more personal symbol. While Augustine saw the Heart as reflecting the secret chamber where divine truth resides, his notion of the Heart was more subjective and based in personal feeling. Instead of viewing the Heart as playing a divine role, he saw it as being subject to storms, conflicts of passion, and feelings arising from the unconscious. Augustine also felt that the Heart housed a person's inner darkness and suffering. Consequently, in his thinking, it lost its aspect of detachment and connection with the divine, taking on a more personal, emotional, and wounded quality.

Within Christian mysticism, one of the most powerful images is the "Sacred Heart of Jesus." Throughout Christian writings, likely beginning around the eleventh century, the image of the pierced Heart has been a symbol of God's love and a source of spiritual contemplation. In the twelfth century, Saint Gertrude had a vision in which she rested her head on Jesus' wounded side and heard the beating of his Heart. Later, in the seventeenth century, a French nun had similar visions, which featured the disembodied, wounded Heart of Jesus. In these visions, the blood from Jesus' pierced Heart becomes the source of nourishment for the followers of the Church. The Christian's devotion to the divine Heart and spiritual life is linked to Jesus' suffering and woundedness, and the Heart of Jesus reflects his divine and infinite love for humankind.

In the present day, we seem to have lost the spiritual connection that other cultures, especially Eastern cultures, have associated with the Heart. Since the Enlightenment and the proclamation of the philosopher René Descartes ("I think; therefore, I am."). Modern Western culture has split two important human psychological functions: the Mind and the Heart. The Mind reflects a certain detached intellect; reason and thinking are highly valued. The Heart, in this view, merely "feels," in a sentimental, highly emotional, or passionate way. Meanwhile, disorders of the heart, a leading cause of death in the Western world, are treated by modern medicine as if they were problems with a machine, a machine that can be routinely replaced just as one would replace a defective part in an automobile.

While there has been some loss of the spiritual connection to the Heart and to Eros, traces of a deeper symbolic meaning remain within the language. When we want to approach the core or centre of something, we say that it is the "heart of the matter." Psychological insight can be integrated into the fabric of our being only when it is "taken to heart." As such, the Heart can be the gateway to the spiritual or divine dimension of life, and contains knowledge of truth that goes beyond personal interests.

The oldest civilizations of the ancient world—the Chinese, the Indians, and the Egyptians—were well aware of this. The myths of these civilizations reveal an image of the Heart that is closely linked with Jung's ideas about conscience and the "Voice of God." In these cosmologies, the Heart is divine and detached. It transcends personal emotions, to reveal a higher knowledge that guides individual behaviour and actions. In this way, the Heart closely supports the process of individuation.

Chinese Hsin: The Heart-Mind

Early Chinese philosophers saw the Heart as the place where people thought and felt. It was the centre that contained Logos and Eros, thinking and feeling. The concept of Heart-Mind, or *Hsin*, comprised the concepts of consciousness and conscience, and it was the focus for cultivating and perfecting the Self or achieving moral perfection. *Hsin* also means "disposition." The best-known Confucian writer to explore this in depth was Mencius.

Mencius, also known as Meng K'o and Meng Tzu, was called the "Second Sage" after Confucius. He lived in the century following Confucius and was educated in the Confucian tradition. The disintegration of the Chinese society to which Confucius had responded continued through to the next century, and China's social and political chaos was barely contained by a legalistic and essentially amoral philosophy that relied heavily on the application of rewards and punishments. Mencius went against the general philosophical trend of the day, advocating the idea that humans are essentially moral beings. The state of the country compelled him to rearticulate Confucian thought within a more systematic philosophical framework and to rethink the concept of morality and its origins.

To Mencius, the importance of the Heart lay in its ability to think. Its thinking was a special kind of thinking—an ethical thinking which established priorities, assigned values, discerned duties, and recognized obligations, "all with a sense of purpose in life—that destiny that is the Mandate of Heaven .... Cultivating the heart is therefore the highest duty because it has the greatest moral value."[16] Unlike the Augustinian image, this Heart is free from desire and emotions.

Mencius' notion of *Hsin* contained four elements: compassion for the suffering of others (*ts'e yin*); shame at the realization that one's actions do not measure up to one's ideals (*hsiu wu*); courtesy and modesty, which reflect the balance between self-interest and self-seeking (*tz'u jang*); and the ability to differentiate between right and wrong (*shih fei*). Each element is an object

16   Elton Hall, *Great Teacher Series—Mencius* (Silver Spring, MD: Theosophy Library
       Online), p. 3 of 5, www. theosophy.org.

of development, and Mencius believed that the "man in whom *Hsin* is fully aroused is a Sage, and who cultivates the heart assiduously is a *chun tzu*. To allow the heart to lie dormant is to be a small person, and to lose the heart through ossification is to become a brute."[17] Mencius recognized that the cultivation of the four elements of the Heart would conflict with self-interest: the *chun tzu* is the person who focuses his or her attention on the Heart within and not on what he or she cannot control in the external world.

> "A gentleman, *chun tzu*," Mencius says, "differs from other men in that he retains his heart." For Mencius, the distinguishing feature of the human being is *Hsin*, the heart, which is not a physical organ but the embryo of a moral possibility and the capacity to fulfill one's *ming*. Because one is born with *Hsin*, he called it the "original heart" and the "true heart." Like a muscle or mental capacity which is never exercised, *Hsin* can atrophy and be lost. Hence the heart must be nurtured and sustained, and all learning serves the sole purpose of "going after this strayed heart. The exceptional nature of the heart lies in its capacity to think, which is the ability to respond to the world without being enslaved to the principle of attraction and repulsion."[18]

According to Mencius, a *chun tzu* is the individual who follows the Way and knows the Mandate of Heaven. For Mencius, the Mandate of Heaven (*Tien-Ming*) represented destiny or the individuation path. As one writer put it, "This view rests on the conception of human nature which allows for intention, choice and change. Hence the unspoken assumption of Confucius that human nature is at root moral, became for Mencius, the central thesis of all Confucian thought."[19] A *chun tzu* is also the person who possesses *jen*. For Confucians, *jen* was the human being's innate moral disposition, but *jen* also has a deeper meaning. It symbolizes a relationship to the divine, which, once awakened, stimulates the need for further cultivation. *Jen* therefore connects to the Heart's divinity. Taken from the perspective of individuation, the Heart articulates the innate path of the Self, the unfolding of one's life path, and growth. *Tien Ming* is "the teleological meaning of the Self and the archetypal constellation of Individuation."[20]

---

17   *Ibid.*, p. 4 of 5.

18   *Ibid.*, p. 3 of 5.

19   *Ibid.*, p. 2 of 5.

20   Rhi, B.Y., "Heaven's Decree: Confucian Contribution to Individuation" in *Proceedings of the 12th Congress of the International Association for Analytical Psychology* (Chicago, 1992), p. 305.

Anahata Chakra

In India, the Heart is considered to be the place of *Brahma*, and it is part of an intricate energy system in the human body. Energy centres known as *chakras* are distinct centres of energy and levels of consciousness within the body. The name *chakra* means wheel or disk in Sanskrit. In this system of seven energy centres, the Heart or *Anahata chakra* is the fourth *chakra*, and it represents the mid-point between the lower three *chakras* and the three above. The lower three are the root support (*Muladhara*); the second *chakra*, which represents lunar feeling and emotional waters (*Swadhistthana*); and the third, which is the place of the will, force, and fire (*Manipura*). Above the heart are the throat *chakra* (*Visuddha*), the place of creative expression and communication; the third eye of true seeing, dreams, and visions (*Ajna*); and the seventh centre of direct awareness and cosmic consciousness (*Sahasrara*). Each represents a further step in the development of consciousness, a new world of consciousness.

It is believed that at the base of the spine lies the *Kundalini* snake curled up, dormant and waiting to be awakened. The catalyst for the spiritual development of consciousness is the ascent of the *Kundalini* through a process of conscious spiritual development. Jung saw this energy as "… 'a microcosmic manifestation of the primordial energy or *Shakti*. It is the Universal Power as it connects the finite body-mind.' The object is to awaken *Kundalini* through ritual practices and to enable her ascent up the *susumna nadi* through the *chakra* system."[21] He was particularly fascinated by this idea because of the lack of a comparable tradition in the West.

The Heart *chakra* reflects the centre of compassion, altruism, forgiveness, and acceptance. In the Hindu tradition, it is in the Heart that love manifests, giving us a sense of responsibility and pure behaviour toward others. The word *Anahata* means, "unstruck sound." It reflects the element of air and corresponds to the lungs, the heart, the arms, and the hands. Like the Chinese *Hsin*, the element of air is important because it is here that the integration of thought and feeling is possible. Where the lower *chakras* reflect the "whirlpool of passions, of instincts, of desires,"[22] a moment of deep reflection can be achieved in the Heart *chakra*, where one is separate from one's desires or emotions. This *chakra* is the centre of love, universal compassion, and detachment. It is green in colour and corresponds to the Sun and the planet Venus.

---

21   C.G. Jung, *The Psychology of Kundalini Yoga* (Princeton: Princeton University Press, 1996), p. xxv.

22   *Ibid.*, p. 36.

Its image is the Lotus of Twelve Petals. (Twelve is the symbol of wholeness and totality.)

A consciousness centred in the Heart integrates rationality and the intellect with the lower energy centres: the emotions, the will, desires, and passions. Jung highlighted the integrative quality of heart consciousness when he wrote:

> For instance we say "You know it in the head, but you don't know it in the heart." There is an extraordinary distance from the head to the heart, a distance of ten, twenty, thirty years or a whole lifetime. For you can know something in the head for forty years and it may never have touched the heart. But only when you have realized it in the heart, do you begin to take notice of it.[23]

In the same reflection, Jung suggested that there is an equal distance between the third *chakra*, the Solar Plexus, and the fourth, the heart. The development of consciousness from the third to the fourth *chakra* is like the sun rising above the horizon. This is where the *purusa* is born, described in Indian philosophy as a consciousness that embodies the Self-conscious spirit. It is at once both the subject of knowledge and the object of knowledge. It is an eternal, unchanging spirit that is the essence of the human being. Jung writes:

> In *Anahata*, you behold the *purusa*, a small figure that is the divine self, namely, that which is not identical with mere causality, mere nature, a mere release of energy that runs down blindly with no purpose.[24]

Therefore, in this energy centre, there is the awareness of something that is not personal—something transpersonal. It is in the *Anahata* that one discovers the Self and begins to individuate.

Egyptian Hall of Maat

For the ancient Egyptians, the Heart was the centre of the Self, the soul, and the emotions. The name for it was *Ab*, or "heart-soul." The hieroglyph for *Ab* was a dancing figure, and as a verb, the word meant "to dance." This connects to the Egyptian notion that the heartbeat was the dance of life in the body. The Heart was the very locus or centre of the personality and functioned as the witness to the deeds of the individual during his lifetime. It was the seat of

---

23   *Ibid.*, p. 35.
24   *Ibid.*, p. 39.

intelligence, the will, and the emotions. *Sia*, the god of understanding, knowledge of the past, and creative imagination, resided in the Heart. The Heart was also the place for a personal genus (*daemon*) who determined the existence and behaviour of each individual.

The Heart also appears to have been the centre of the senses, the organ that processes sensory data. First-dynasty texts that have been discovered refer to the Heart as the ruler of the soul and the seat of perception:

> The sight of the eyes, the hearing of the ears, and the smelling of the air by the nose, they report to the heart. It is this which causes every completed concept to come forth, and it is the tongue which announces what the heart thinks.[25]

Indeed, according to the Egyptian creation myth, *Ptah*, the God of Creation, first planned the universe in his heart and then expressed his vision through the spoken word, bringing the universe into existence.

In the mummy, the heart was the only part of the viscera that was left because it was considered indispensable to the body in eternity. Maat, the Egyptian Goddess of Judgment, weighed the heart to determine the moral quality of the person. The heart was placed on one side of a scale and an ostrich feather—Maat's symbol of truth and justice—was placed on the other side. In many cultures, the feather is a symbol of ascension and is linked with the afterlife. Feathers worn by kings reflected the fact that heavenly power was delegated to them, but this power entailed taking on responsibility to administer justice. If the heart weighed correctly against the weight of the feather, the person would be considered justified in his or her life, and deemed worthy to join the Gods in the Fields of Peace. The Heart was seen as a symbol of the person's conduct, conscience, and ethical outlook on life. In this ritual in the Hall of Judgment, the individual was judged as to whether they had a "true voice", whether the tongue had said anything with which the Heart had disagreed. In the life of a disciple of one of the sages, it is written, "a man's heart is his own god and my heart is content with my deeds."[26] For the Egyptians, Maat represented the highest conception of physical and moral law and order, and the Heart was the organ of thought, imagination, and truth. In Jungian terms, it functioned as the objective psyche.

---

25   George Elder, *The Body: Encyclopaedia of Archetypal Symbolism* (Boston, MA: Shambhala Publications, 1997), p. 299.

26   Jean Chevalier, *Dictionary of Symbols* (London: Penguin Books, 1996), p. 480.

In his book *Solar Conscience, Lunar Conscience*, Murray Stein sees the weighing of the Heart in Egyptian mythology as a reflection of a lunar conscience, a "mother right," which he defines as a sense of order and law that exists within the realm of Nature itself. This connection is embedded in the name of the Goddess herself, Maat, which was originally based on the Indo-European syllable for "mother." The Heart becomes the conscience, the "Voice of God" that determines one's fate.

❧

The Heart as Morality and as the Centre of the Personality

As the centre of the body and the psyche, the Heart embodies the connection between God (the divine) and the human realm. It is a point of integration and unity, where the spirit world and the world of matter unite to form the ego-Self axis. This has a great effect on how we experience our own morality, our ethical stance toward the world. It is a relational concept, in which the individual is in a dialectic situation with some Other in any of its forms: another person, another value system, or, internally, the Self. The symbolic representations used in ancient Eastern civilizations may not pertain to modern society directly, but there is enough evidence to suggest that the integrity and authenticity expressed in the Heart reflects an inherent truth within the psyche.

The Heart has its own reasons and its own intelligence, and it has the ability to mediate between the mind and the world as some third element, that is, as an aspect of what Jung called the *transcendent function*.[27] The West has forgotten this Heart. This Heart possesses a high degree of differentiation of feeling, has a teleology (a doctrine of purpose), and is a place of soul and of imagination. It seems to reflect the interdependence between image and love (Eros), and carries the teleological function of the psyche, the drive toward wholeness through this symbolic and imaginal world.

The psychological connection between the Heart and morality is deeply related to the path of individuation. It is also bound up with the process of coming to terms with the Self as the centre of the personality and as a reflection of one's uniqueness, and it is related to the consciousness of universal experiences and knowledge.

---

27   James Hillman, *Eranos Lecture: The Thought of the Heart* (Thalwil, Switzerland: Spring Publications), p. 4.

CHAPTER 5

Individuation and the
Ethical Confrontation with the Unconscious

The years when I pursued the inner images were the most important time
of my life. Everything else is to be derived from this. It began at that time,
and the later details hardly matter anymore. My entire life consisted in
elaborating what had burst forth from the unconscious and flooded me like
an enigmatic stream and threatened to break me. That was the stuff and
material for more than only one life.

—C.G. Jung[1]

The images of the unconscious place a great responsibility upon a man.
Failure to understand them, or a shirking of ethical responsibility, deprives
him of his wholeness and impact a painful fragmentation on his life.

—C.G. Jung[2]

The consideration of Heart knowledge, integrity, and authenticity previously
discussed has a particular relevance to Jung's notion of individuation. The
Heart, as a symbol of the centre of wholeness—the Self—is the place of our
integrity and innate morality. Connected to that, Jung saw individuation as a
natural process of psychological development toward wholeness. Individuation
is therefore the path to the Heart and to our innate morality. However, the
journey to the Heart and our morality also involves a confrontation with the

---

1   C.G. Jung, *The Red Book, Liber Novus*, ed. Sonu Shamdasani (New York: W.W. Norton
      & Company, 2009), back cover.

2   C.G. Jung, *Memories, Dreams, Reflections* (New York: Random House, 1961), p. 177.

"amorality" of the unconscious. This is where Jung's moral imperative comes into play. He understood that, embedded in the individuation process, was the ethical confrontation with the unconscious. This chapter examines the nature of the unconscious and Jung's own confrontation with it after his friendship with Freud ended in 1912. (Since 2009, thanks to the publication of Jung's *Red Book*, we have had access to these images and active imaginations that before were hidden from public view. Until then, Jung's material had been the subject of hearsay, misunderstanding, and projection.)

The paradigm that currently prevails in Western civilization reflects a morality that supports the one-sided values of ego consciousness. They commit to the Shadow aspects of the personality that are at odds with prevailing collective norms. In *Depth Psychology and the New Ethic*, Erich Neumann outlines this dualism and notes how the projection of the Shadow and evil encourages psychological splitting within individuals and collectives. Neumann calls it "the old ethic" or the *ethics of the conscious attitude*,[3] because it fails to consider the effects of the unconscious. Neumann suggests that:

> It is an individualistic ethic since it accepts no responsibility for the unconscious reactions of the group or the collective. That is why the old ethic is inadequate; the compensatory relationship between consciousness and the unconscious, which it fails to take into account, turns out to be a major cause of the contemporary crisis in human affairs and actually the crucial ethical problem of our time.[4]

At a deeper level, the moral courage needed to embark on one's individuation journey is connected to the mystery of the analytical process. This raises many questions: What compels people to embark on some kind of psychological journey, and what causes others not to? What makes it possible for the work to take place? What prevents such work from taking place? Why do some people complete the journey and why do others fall by the wayside? Why do some individuals respond to life-altering situations with growth, while others are crushed by them?

At the root of these questions is a more basic one: What is the "subject" of the individuation process? San Francisco analyst John Beebe suggests that it is not the transformation of character, but the development of integrity. Accord-

---

3   Erich Neumann, *Depth Psychology and the New Ethic* (New York: Harper Torchbooks, 1969), p. 74.

4   *Ibid.*, p. 75.

ing to Beebe, analysis strengthens moral fortitude and the ego, and this, in turn, strengthens the ego-Self axis and the ability to integrate unconscious material. It is through this confrontation with the unconscious that we come to experience more of our authenticity. Jung's works are filled with images and symbols of transformation as the personality strives for wholeness and development, and psychological development is defined as integration of material from the unconscious toward completeness. Alchemical imagery, with its ritualistic notions of symbolic death and rebirth, suggests that through the process of analysis a fundamental change in the personality might be achieved.

The Nature of the Unconscious

With the discovery of the unconscious in the late 19th century, a new realm of understanding about human nature emerged. New problems and dilemmas also surfaced, however—both individual and collective. Especially at deeper levels of the psyche, the energy within the unconscious has tremendous power and can pull consciousness into its field. Jung felt that this state of being was like a "possession," where the unconscious takes over the ego and the individual loses her conscious identity and the power of discrimination. The ego then becomes the victim of an autonomous complex that removes the power of choice and of will, and moves the individual to behave in uncharacteristic ways. If it is an archetype that possesses the ego, the risk is then an inflation or, at worst, psychosis.

The idea that there exists in human beings an innate morality has been referred to many times in these pages. It is an idea that Jung subscribed to. But is the unconscious moral or ethical? Jung also concluded that the unconscious is amoral, not moral or ethical, and is therefore duplicitous and dangerous. He saw that the spirit of Mercurius—the Trickster image from alchemy—was the ruler of the unconscious,[5] meaning that the unconscious has the potential to be creative or destructive, light or dark, good or evil, moral or immoral. Its duplicity means that it needs to be handled with care.

Since the psyche's innate morality does not reside in the unconscious, we must look elsewhere to find it. We can begin with the compensatory aspect of the unconscious, its relationship to consciousness, and the attitude of the ego toward the unconscious. The valuations of good and evil originate in the ego, that is, from consciousness, not from the unconscious. Theories of moral devel-

---

5   Murray Stein, "Introduction" in *Jung on Evil* (Princeton,. NJ: Princeton University Press, 1996), p. 6.

opment tell us that the ego has responsibility for making subjective judgements and is the keeper of individual values. More sophisticated moral judgements also come with higher levels of consciousness. When unconscious archetypes or complexes overtake a person, the individual enters a state of *participation mystique* ("mystical participation") in which they *identify* with the complex or archetype. When this happens, they lose their ability to make an ethical determination. It is only through distance that the ethical state can be experienced, and because moral valuation is an ego function, it is through the ego, in its detachment, that an ethical state can be experienced.

Jung's Confrontation with the Unconscious

In the years between 1906 and 1912, Jung was actively engaged in supporting and promoting Freud's new discipline of psychoanalysis. Freud's vision of psychology was innovative and subject to much controversy at the time. Throughout this period, although his relationship with Freud became quite close, Jung felt a growing disagreement with certain aspects of Freud's dogmatic approach. Even though both men espoused the need for compromise and collegial dialogue, it was apparent a chasm existed that could not be bridged. Freud was notorious for cutting people off who did not agree with his theory wholeheartedly, and he was growing tired of Jung's alternative views. He initiated the end to their personal relationship in a letter dated January 3, 1913. Jung's letter in response ended with, "and the rest is silence."

In *Memories, Dreams, Reflections*, Jung relates that, following his break with Freud, he experienced feelings of uncertainty and disorientation. The loss was personal, but Jung also feared for his professional future.[6] Jung struggled with a paradox: a strong identification with the psychoanalytic movement as defined by Freud, along with a powerful need to work with his patients in a different way and with a new attitude. This experience caused a psychological "disturbance," which he suspected might be related to an unresolved issue from his past. In order to learn more about the source of this disturbance, he "consciously submitted [himself] to the impulses of the unconscious."[7] He had decided that it was his personal obligation to explore his own psyche.

During the process, Jung resurrected writing in the "black books," which he had abandoned in 1902. In doing so, "an incessant stream of fantasies" was released, as he says. In an approach that was a common practice for the time,

---

6   Deirdre Bair, *Jung: A Biography* (New York: Back Bay Books, 2004), p. 241.
7   C.G. Jung, *Memories, Dreams Reflections* (New York: Random House, 1961), p. 173.

Jung had embarked on a self-experiment of introspection to understand what the images, fantasies and visions that came to him were about. In his inner landscape, Jung had activated the unconscious through building-games and fantasies he explored in his "play." He recorded his dialogues with the figures from the unconscious in black books (which he then transfer into a heftier volume with a red leather cover that he had especially commissioned).

During his confrontation with the unconscious, Jung was bombarded with psychic storms, eruptions of negative emotions, and a stream of images and fantasies. Shamdasani describes them as "a type of dramatized thinking in pictorial form," revealing Jung's fascination with the world of myth and epic.[8] Jung would later call the process *active imagination*. His first active imagination was in November, 1913, and he continued over the next several months.

During that year, the psychological pressure grew in intensity, originating from both outside and inside his psyche. In the fall of 1913, three psychological experiences were the catalysts for a "descent"[9]; they were at once personal and influenced by the growing political tensions in Europe. In *The Black Books*, Jung wrote down several visions and dreams that he found disturbing and baffling. After some reflection, the images that he at first thought were personal, he came to conclude were unconscious perceptions of increasing collective tensions. Jung believed that the language these images were using, and which he tried to capture, was the language of archetypes. He recognized that they had energy far superior to the strength of his ego. He wrote:

> My enduring these storms was a question of brute strength. Others have been shattered by them—Nietzsche, and Hölderlin, and many others. But there was a demonic strength in me, and from the beginning there was no doubt in my mind that I must find the meaning of what I was experiencing in these fantasies. When I endured these assaults of the unconscious, I had an unswerving conviction that I was obeying a higher will, and that feeling continued to uphold me until I had mastered the task.[10]

In encountering these strange inner images, Jung met with a great deal of resistance and fear within himself. Because of his psychiatric training, he knew that he was at risk of being overwhelmed and falling into a psychosis, and he was acutely aware that he was treading on dangerous ground. It was

---

8   Sonu Shamdasani, *C.G. Jung's Liber Novus*, Introduction, p. 200.
9   Bair, *Jung*, p. 242.
10   Jung, *Memories, Dreams, Reflections*, p. 177.

his outer world, as a professional with a family, that kept him firmly in reality. Indeed, according to the historical account of Jung's life at that time,[11] Jung was able to partition these activities: his outer life was busy with a full practice, professional meetings, family responsibilities and military service, while his evenings were spent dedicated to self-explorations.[12]

What is important in the description of these experiences is Jung's ego attitude toward what surfaced. In many of his encounters with the unconscious, either through dreams or in his active imaginations, Jung was confronted with ideas or images that challenged his ego ideals and attitudes. He felt devalued and embarrassed by what he unearthed in the process. He wrote that he experienced emotions "of which I could not approve" and had fantasies that "often struck me as nonsense." It would have been easy for him to dismiss his moral obligation to understand these images by considering them only as minor passing perceptions.

The result of Jung's descent was a powerful personal text in the visionary tradition of William Blake and Emanuel Swedenborg,[13] which combined hand-painted images, active imaginations and a commentary.

Jung's emergence from the darkness coincided with the end of the war, and at that point, he was confronted with a choice. The work he had done with the dreams and fantasies meant that the academic world no longer interested him, and the insights that had arisen from his unconscious were too confusing, too new, and too fragile to share with his colleagues and students. Feeling that he could not retain his position at the university, Jung wrote:

> I therefore felt that I was confronted with the choice of either continuing my academic career, whose road lay smooth before me, or following the laws of my inner personality, of a higher reason, and forging ahead with this curious task of mine, this experiment in confrontation with the unconscious.[14]

Jung's decision was also based on what he considered to be his ethical responsibility to encourage the individuation process. He felt it was not enough only to observe—he also had a moral imperative to bring the fruits of the unconscious to life:

> I took great care to try to understand every single image ... and above all,

---

11   *Ibid.*, p. 201.
12   *Ibid.*
13   Sonu Shamdasani, C.G. Jung *Red Book Symposium*, Library of 6-19-10.
14   Jung, *Memories, Dreams, Reflections*, p. 193.

to realize them in actual life. We allow the images to rise and maybe we wonder about them, but that is all. We do not take the trouble to understand them, let alone draw ethical conclusions from them. This stopping short conjures up the negative effects of the unconscious. ... It is equally a grave mistake to think that it is enough to gain some understanding of the images and that knowledge can here make a halt. Insight into them must be converted into an ethical obligation. Not to do so is to fall prey to the power principle, and this produces dangerous effects which are destructive not only to others but even to the knower. The images of the unconscious place a great responsibility upon a man. Failure to understand them, or a shirking of ethical responsibility, deprives him of his wholeness and imposes a painful fragmentation on his life.[15]

The product of this period of self-reflection and experimentation is *Liber Novus* or *The Red Book*. The volume reflects a process of transformation and renewal depicting the rebirth of the God-image in the soul, and an attempt by Jung to recreate his personal cosmology.[16] *The Red Book* was Jung's experiment in allowing the unconscious to question our values and the directions of our lives. Specifically, in the early pages, Jung identifies two pulls in his life—one is what he called the "Spirit of the Times" and the other, the "Spirit of the Depths." Through this process, Jung emerges from identification with collective values creates his own path or way. And, most importantly, he emerges with a new and innovative vision for psychology.

The Red Book is a reflection of the spiritual alienation of our time, and it would become a prototype of the process Jung would later call *individuation*. He worked on the book for sixteen years, but was apparently deeply ambivalent about publishing it because he believed it wouldn't be accepted. He stopped working on it after he was introduced to alchemy and received a copy of Richard Wilhelm's translation of the ancient Chinese *Secret of the Golden Flower*. However, Jung's self-experiment did mark a change in how he practiced. He encouraged his patients to embark on similar processes and to record their active imaginations, dialogues and images in their own journals. Two organizations, the Association for Analytical Psychology and the Psychology Club, were founded in Zurich during this time, and Jung participated to a large extent. They became vehicles for others to explore, in a collegial context, some of the ideas arising from Jung's descent into the unconscious.

---

15   *Ibid.*
16   Shamdasani, *C.G. Jung's Liber Novus*, Introduction, p. 202.

Individuation

Jung believed in the vital importance of the process of individuation. But what did he mean by that concept? His choice of the word *individuation* derives from his reading of the philosopher Schopenhauer,[17] who used the term *principium individuationis* to refer to a person's separation from the chaos of life while under the protective watch of the god Apollo. For Jung, individuation reflected, first and foremost, a process of differentiation and self-realization by which the individual finds her uniqueness and potential, becoming the person she was meant to be. This is accomplished through the experience of her own personality and in relationship with others. Jung writes: "Individuation means becoming an 'in-dividual' and in so far as 'individuality' embraces our innermost, last, and incomparable uniqueness, it also implies becoming one's own self. We could therefore translate individuation as 'coming to selfhood' or 'self-realization.'"[18]

It is important to acknowledge that the individuation process is never completed but is ongoing throughout life. The unconscious consistently reinforces the fact that there are things that live and function in the psyche of which the ego is unaware. Thus the ego in such a system is not ruler of the psyche but merely the centre of consciousness, and individuation implies a process of integration of the contents of the unconscious with consciousness. This moves us toward wholeness and leads to our experience of a more authentic Self.

The process of individuation also includes knowing something of God's nature and the religious and spiritual dimensions of the psyche. To illustrate this point, Jung examined the Christian myth in such a way that it could be viewed as a symbolic depiction of the individuation process. In his book, *C.G. Jung's Psychology of Religion and Synchronicity*, Robert Aziz highlights this very important distinction when he writes:

> The myth of the Incarnation of God, the suffering of the God-man in this world, his crucifixion and resurrection is, Jung sought to demonstrate, a living archetypal drama that is actually being enacted in the lives of all of us. From the Jungian perspective, this archetypal drama so magnifi-

---

17   Andrew Samuels, Bani Shorter, and Fred Plaut, *Critical Dictionary of Jungian Analysis* (London: Routledge, 1986), p. 76.

18   C.G. Jung, *Two Essays on Analytical Psychology*, Vol. 7 of *The Collected Works* (Princeton, NJ: Princeton University Press, 1966), paragraph 266.

cently depicted in the Christian Myth is indeed the ongoing struggle of the conscious and the unconscious, the ego and the self. It is at once the suffering and the joy associated with both the ego's struggle for higher levels of consciousness and the self's relentless desire for incarnation in this life.[19]

The Shadow and Psychological Development

To embark on an individuation journey invariably results in the ego's ideals and perceptions being challenged when the ego is confronted with the totality of the personality and the boundless realm of the unconscious.[20] Much courage is needed to face the Shadow, and thus to undertake the individuation process. Although others often see the Shadow clearly, the person who is confronted with it in themselves is not consciously aware of its existence. This is because the Shadow is formed from qualities that have been repressed as the individual has favoured some personality characteristics over others. The Shadow is further hidden from the individual because it is a portion of the whole Self that the ego considers bad or evil because of shame, social pressure, and family and societal attitudes.[21]

It is our experience of the Shadow that tests our ethical approach to the development of our personality. Intra-psychically, it reflects the least developed and neglected parts of our personality. When these reach the light of day, they can be experienced by the ego as evil, infantile, ugly, or sick, and the ego's encounter with these repressed aspects results in feelings of shame, guilt, and embarrassment. It is these uncomfortable negative emotions that initiate repressing mechanisms such as denial, projection, and suppression.

In Jung's conception of the psychological journey, integration or assimilation of the Shadow represents the beginning of the individuation process. But what does this mean? If the definition of integrity or integration is applied, it means that we begin a psychological process to accept our imperfection and to take responsibility for aspects of our personality that we have disowned. Ownership of our Shadow represents a move toward greater integrity and leads to authenticity and wholeness. This is a lifelong process. As one older analyst once told me, she experienced herself gaining more authenticity and genuineness as she progressed through life.

---

19   Robert Aziz, *C.G. Jung's Psychology of Religion and Synchronicity* (Albany: State University of New York Press, 1990), p. 43.
20   Neumann, *Depth Psychology*, p. 77.
21   Stein, "Introduction," in *Jung on Evil*, p. 9.

Tests of our integrity come when we feel emotions of personal need that live in the Shadow areas of our consciousness: fear, desire, hunger, fatigue, anger, or pain. We are challenged to move to a more sophisticated morality when we see that we have been using denial or self-deception to push the Shadow away. Because the person has not accepted the Shadow or, on a collective level, has repressed what is perceived as an evil threatening all of society, the confrontation with the Shadow puts the entire person or society into question. From this perspective, one might say that immorality or the unethical can be found in a person whose self-deception denies the existence of the Shadow and who fails to work on bringing its aspects into full consciousness.

Our culture and the dominant interpretation of Christianity have encouraged us to take on an attitude of fear and acquire a victim psychology. Following the dictates of this ethos, it is common for us to blame and to project the problems of our lives on outside influences—including other people, circumstances, the environment, or genetics. This attitude represents an abdication of our power and control. It is also an abdication of responsibility, as the ego maintains a false innocence. Psychologically, this might be experienced as a feeling of powerlessness and inability to confront the blows that life may bring. This is especially true in cases where the individual identifies with the collective and there is no differentiation between the ego and the persona (that is, the mask we show to the world).

Integrity as the Opus

What is the purpose or "subject" of the individuation process? Images and symbols of transformation permeate Jung's writings, reflecting Jung's personality in its striving for wholeness and development. Alchemical imagery, with its ritualistic notions of symbolic death and rebirth, suggests that through the process of analysis, a fundamental change in the personality can be achieved. This would imply that the purpose of the individuation process is the transformation of character. This discussion is based on the work of John Beebe, a San Francisco analyst who suggests that it is in fact the development of integrity that is the opus of the work—not specifically the transformation of character. However, transformation of character, particularly moral character, may indeed result from the pursuit of integrity, from the ongoing struggle and tension between aspects of one's embodied or innate nature. As Beebe writes:

> What can individuate out of a person's character is integrity, that accountability for the impact of the self upon others which makes the work on

the rest of character—recognizing it, allowing for it, compensating for it, training it—possible.[22]

If character is body, integrity is spirit. Integrity is the paradoxical combination of vulnerability and confidence that makes work on character possible. We cannot find our integrity, however, until we know our character, which is one reason why even a psychotherapy, which seems to stumble on the limitations imposed by particular complexes frequently strengthens integrity and fosters the sense of individuation.[23]

The Psychological Experience of Integrity and Conscience

History reveals that some individuals have felt compelled to follow a higher inner moral order—often at the cost of their personal safety, and even though their actions go against collective ideals. Conscientious objectors and Mahatma Gandhi are examples. In a captivating development in the myth of Oedipus, his daughter, Antigone, attempts to redeem the consequences of her father's and grandfather's actions. The play opens with her return to Thebes after her father's death, to find that her two brothers, Polyneices and Eteocles, have fought over the kingdom and killed one another. Their uncle, Creon, has become king, and refuses to bury Polyneices, who is to remain where he has fallen while his brother receives full burial with honour. Creon even decrees that no one may touch Polyneices' body, on pain of death. Antigone is torn between two unyielding demands: if she obeys the collective decree, she will dishonour her ancestors and the sacred laws set down to honour the dead, and if she buries her brother, the collective will stone her. Antigone's allegiance is to a higher moral order that transcends the collective decree, as is evident in the speech she directs to her sister at the beginning of the play:

> … I shall bury him.
> And if I have to die for this pure crime, I am
> content, for I shall rest beside him;
> His love will answer mine. I have to please
> The dead far longer than I need to please

---

22 John Beebe, "Toward a Jungian Analysis of Character," in *Post-Jungians Today: Key Papers in Contemporary Analytical Psychology*, ed. Ann Casement (London: Routledge, 1998). Also on www.cgjungpage.org, p. 9 of 18.

23 *Ibid.*, p. 9.

The living; with them, I have to dwell forever.
But you, if so choose, you may dishonour
The sacred laws that Heaven holds in honour.[24]

Such a compulsion to follow one's own sense of right and wrong is often a necessary precondition for social reform. For James Q. Wilson, author of *The Moral Sense*,[25] a moral person is someone who not only honours his obligations but is also disposed to do so when it is not in his interest to do so. While it is true that certain moral behaviour is motivated by negative consequences related to losing love, companionship, or loyalty, sufficient research exists to suggest that something else is at work.

Psychological studies conducted in the 1960s explored the motivation behind benevolent or altruistic behaviour. Researchers tested the willingness of people to respond to victims in need during various types of emergencies. The findings showed that it was more likely for a lone bystander to rise to the call than for a group of onlookers to come to a victim's aid. It seemed, therefore, that a sense of conscience does not materialize when there is safety in numbers. These studies confirmed that social recognition does not motivate "good Samaritans" to take action in the face of human suffering. In fact, the findings suggested that social context and group pressure play a significant role in inhibiting altruistic behaviour.

Similar findings were uncovered in a study of Europeans who helped Jews avoid Nazi concentration camps during the Second World War. These heroic acts were not motivated by material reward, and they often resulted in the rescuers putting their own lives in danger. These people were more likely to be motivated by ethical factors that originated in sympathy and compassion for the victims. Every one of the Europeans interviewed had had a first-hand experience of deep human suffering, and this gave them a strong sense of principles and humanity, which compelled them to act. The studies suggested that Eros and compassion strongly influence acts of conscience. This knowledge resides in the Heart—compassion strong enough to initiate action, though personal costs are high.

As mentioned in Chapter 4, integrity is a psychological phenomenon more than a philosophical one, as psychological experiences inform us of our integrity or conscience. If integrity is the voice of conscience, it has an elusive quality that defies clear description, except through the experience of psycho-

---

24   Sophocles, *Antigone* (Oxford: Oxford University Press, 1962), p. 5.
25   James Q. Wilson, *A Moral Sense* (New York: The Free Press, 1993).

logical symptoms such as guilt, shame, outrage, torment, and human suffering. Guilt, for instance, may suggest the violation of societal norms, which results in social anxiety or fear of isolation from the group. This motivates us to live within what is expected of us as citizens of a larger collective context.

In a sense, integrity is an archetype. John Beebe uses Jung's theories of typology to define the psychological experience of integrity, suggesting that

> in practical terms, anyone who is able to establish a living connection between superior function and inferior function, and thus establish a bond between ego and Self can feel their integrity on an ongoing basis. It becomes a center out of which ethical discriminations can be made and ethical relations with inner and outer objects established.[26]

The breakdown of the ego–Self axis cripples the ethical capacities of the personality. Such a breakdown means that an individual has lost the connection to his genuineness and his integrity. This is an important distinction to make because of the power that complexes and archetypal energy have to overpower the ego and break the connection to the centre.

The relevance of analytical psychology is directly felt in our subjective experiences and in our experience of integrity. Our emotions are the indicators of this. According to Beebe, the psychological experience of integrity is something that we delight in and is self-validating. It is the feeling of being centred and balanced. Such an experience involves the relativization of the ego in relation to the Self—that is, a recognition that the ego is not the sole master of its house, that it is contained in something larger. To come to this realization, it is necessary to consciously serve the greater centre of the personality—the Self—and to take on the required tasks. The ego, with its desires and wishes, submits to the higher moral authority of integrity, conscience, and the Self. This results in a feeling of Eros and relatedness to something Other. It is the felt sense of "knowing" and "experiencing" that Jung tried to articulate—the "Yes!" of inner knowing, the sense that "*This* is the decision to be made." It is also about taking a risk, and with risk comes responsibility because one could be wrong. After all, it could be the "Voice of the Devil" that one is following and not the "Voice of God."

Doubt, anxiety, and a state of psychological dis-ease are sometimes the signals that we are out of balance, that the natural state of psychic equilibrium

---

26   John Beebe, "Jung Seminar with John Beebe, M.D., June 16–18, 2000", sponsored by www.cgjungpage.org, e-mail to author, June 17, 2000.

is not present, that we have lost connection with our integrity and wholeness. When this happens, conscience creates a psychological state of ambivalence. Some event or situation, or an intra-psychic conflict between the ego and some Other, is constellated, where resolution requires an expansion of awareness beyond ego consciousness. This Other reflects an ideal, a principle, a value, or a standard of behaviour by which one evaluates actions. Our feeling of anxiety or our depression may suggest that we have violated some inner law. The unfortunate part is that because these feelings are usually uncomfortable, we tend to ignore or repress them.

Jungian analyst Robert Bosnak explored the notion of whether human beings possess a deeper sense that enables them to distinguish between good and bad behaviour. He identified an ethical instinct, which is felt viscerally (in the body). Collective moral codes and systems are therefore built upon human beings' ability to feel abhorrence and disgust. Similar to the body, which reacts to foreign substances that can create disease, the psyche has a rejection mechanism that is experienced as revulsion or abhorrence when we encounter notions or actions that are morally foreign to our being. In other words, the emotional reaction to violation is an instinctive response.

Murray Stein would tend to agree with this interpretation. The experience of our consciousness, he says, is less a matter of conscious reflection and more "an instinctive sense and knowledge of the difference between good and evil."[27] This instinctual knowledge corresponds to his concept of a lunar conscience. Mythologically, this appears in the Furies or in the goddess Nemesis—figures who inflict sickness, madness or death upon those who violate laws of Nature or the plan of life that rests in kinship, attachment, and relatedness. Conscience, according to Stein, is founded in Eros and requires acceptance of life. It serves to remind us of our humanity. It is this conscience that can be found in the Heart—in what Jung describes as the "Voice of God."

It is also possible to experience our integrity in circumstances where our conscience feels something loathsome, foreign, and alien to our values and our truth. This can result in a physical sense of revulsion, and can manifest as anxiety, anger, rage, or outrage. Our need to correct the situation is aroused, whether we are the victim or the perpetrator of the wrong. Outrage, according to Robert Bosnak, is "one of the most valuable capacities we have. Outrage is the ethical response to intolerable situations that can lead to passionate

---

27   Murray Stein, *Solar Conscience, Lunar Conscience* (Wilmette, Ill: Chiron Publications, 1993), p. 4.

action."[28] Rage at a violation as an outward expression of conscience does not arise from calm deliberation, idealism, or empathy, but it does frequently override self-interest and leads to the admission of guilt. This body reaction suggests that conscience is also instinctual and is expressed physically as a kind of intelligence—an instinctive knowledge of what is right, good, and moral. Bosnak writes: "Nature is amoral and so is natural man. But a man of conscience is able to feel sick of his own natural reactions and to muster an instinctive response against greed and self-interest that is strong enough to [help him] come to a moral decision. Only our instinctive sense of ethics is strong enough to overrule our immediate self-interest."[29]

Ethical Confrontation with the Unconscious and the "New Ethic"

Jung's own experiences, originating with the image of the turd falling on the cathedral roof when he was eleven and including his confrontation with the unconscious at mid-life, reveal a struggle to find his own path that was not consistent with his Christian upbringing. The key to finding this path lay in the moral obligation to listen and work with the messages of the unconscious. Morality, to him, was synonymous with responsibility. In the foreword to *Depth Psychology and the New Ethic*, he wrote: "Although every act of conscious realization is at least a step forward on the road to individuation, to the 'making whole' of the individual, the integration of the personality is unthinkable without the responsible, and that means moral, relation of the parts to one another."[30]

It is a moral obligation that comes from deep within the personality—the source of virtuous behaviour that is individual and subjective. It is the moral obligation to cultivate one's genuineness and authenticity. This task demands a partnership between the ego and the Self. The ego is the object of the moral act, for the ego is in the world. At the same time, the Self is "supra ordinate" to the ego and demands that ego surrender its will to the higher will of Self. Both ego and Self are needed. Jung says elsewhere that:

So long as the Self is unconscious, it corresponds to Freud's superego and

---

28   Robert Bosnak, "Ethical Instinct" in *Asian and Jungian View of Ethics* (Westport: Greenwood Press, 1999), p. 59.

29   *Ibid.*, p. 49.

30   C.G. Jung, "Foreword to Neumann: *Depth Psychology and the New Ethic*" in *The Symbolic Life*, Vol. 18 of *The Collected Works* (Princeton, NJ: Princeton University Press, 1976), paragraph 412.

is a source of perpetual moral conflict. If, however, it is withdrawn from projection and is no longer identical with public opinion, then one is truly one's own yea or nay. The Self then functions as a union of opposites, and thus constitutes the most immediate experience of the Divine, which it is psychologically possible to imagine.[31]

It would be easy to dismiss Jung's argument as supporting moral relativism: "Everything goes" as long as you are true to yourself and your own individuation path. It is true that a moral ethic of doing your own thing can be an easy justification for narcissism, but I do not believe that this was Jung's intention. Actions and behaviour bear consequences. Err in favour of either side of the equation—collective moral standards or individual path and conscience—and an *enantiodromia*[32] will constellate from either the unconscious or the collective. Murray writes:

> The conscious struggle to come to a moral decision is for Jung the prerequisite for what he calls ethics, the action of the whole person, the self. If this work is left undone, the individual and society as a whole will suffer .... To be ethical is work, and it is the essential human task. Human beings cannot look "above" for what is right and wrong, good or evil; we must struggle with these questions and recognize that, while there are no clear answers, it is still crucial to continue probing further and refining our judgements more precisely. This is an endless process of moral reflection. And the price for getting it wrong can be catastrophic.[33]

The moral problem of the Shadow is of concern both to collectives and to individuals. Individuation as an ethical process implies taking responsibility for our suffering and our healing, and the acceptance of the boundary between personal responsibility and events that are outside of our control. Psychological process means that, as individuals, we take responsibility for our own actions, thoughts, and wishes in creating our emotional world. As Erich Neumann writes, "in the end, the individual is brought face to face with the necessity for 'accepting' his own evil."[34]

---

31   C.G. Jung, *Psychology and Religion: West and East*, Vol. 11 of *The Collected Works* (Princeton, NJ: Princeton University Press, 1969), paragraph 396.

32   The term *enantiodromia*, first coined by Heraclitus, means that everything sooner or later turns into its opposite.

33   Stein, "Introduction" in *Jung on Evil*, p. 10.

34   Neumann, *Depth Psychology*, p. 80.

In contrast to the Judeo-Christian "old ethic," Neumann's *new ethic* has as its orientation the totality of the personality and the orientation toward wholeness and integration. Its principal aim is to transcend the opposites and arrive at a synthesis. Here, the ethical obligation is to become conscious and to withdraw what one has projected onto others and the environment. According to this ideal, the ego becomes healthy and productive and not psychologically dangerous to other people. It is self-contained, and this allows the person to accept moral responsibility for her own negative material.

There are two orientations—outer and inner. Both, in fact, are needed. The first orientation assumes that the individual's ethical attitude has an effect on the collective and that the individual has a role in the collective or the group. The second includes reckoning the effect of the conscious attitude on the unconscious. Intra-psychically, the two work in tandem. The individual must first work through his own basic moral Shadow problem before he is in a position to play a responsible part in the collective.[35] Neumann proposes that "the new ethic is based on an attempt to become conscious of both the positive and negative forces in the human organism and to relate these forces consciously to the life of the individual and the community."[36]

With the ethical responsibility of awareness and consciousness, the ego's mediating role becomes paramount. The ego thus becomes the authority to manage the relationship between the unconscious and the conscious mind. According to Neumann, truth becomes more important than notions of good and bad: "The decisive factor from the ethical point of view is now the criterion of truth. In this context, the fact and the extent of self-awareness emerge as a value in the ethical not in the scientific sense of that term."[37]

Truth is "one's subjective psychic truth," which comes from full consciousness of the impact of one's decisions on the people around you and the environment. With this, the individual can now become oriented toward wholeness, the middle way, a process of integration where the personality structure does not regress into the conflict of opposites. At the same time, our ability to be in the world is strengthened and deepened.

৵

Our ethical confrontation with ourselves first means allowing the emotions and feelings to surface, no matter how uncomfortable, distasteful or unpleas-

---

35   *Ibid.*, p. 93.
36   *Ibid.*, p. 94.
37   *Ibid.*, p. 114.

ant they are. The existence of the Shadow is very painful for the ego. Individuation is about recognizing the truth of oneself, which includes the actual situation of the individual, the causes and meaning of suffering, the patterns of one's life, and the lessons that must be learned. In their book *Religion and the Unconscious*, Ann and Barry Ulanov suggest that individuation is about living a life of value, "a life filled with a sense of being real, of living in close touch with ourselves, with others, with society, with history, and with hope."[38] It requires integrity and strength of character to meet this challenge and to confront the truth in all of its pain. The experience of the truth is accompanied by understanding, compassion, tolerance, and the acceptance of imperfection. It is also about struggling with uncertainty and doubt about the experience of truth itself.

The ethical confrontation with the unconscious has to do with our own subjective experience of the unconscious and how we evaluate its messages. The duplicitous nature of the unconscious means that none of these messages can be approached with any certainty. It is this subjective experience of the unconscious that produces subjective values, and "one's sense of value arises now out of the most personal impression of the influence of the unconscious on every choice one makes, on every action or inaction."[39] Morality rests on values we feel in the Heart—values that come from the deepest part of our personality, from the dialogue between the ego and the Self, and from a union of what we think and how we feel. These values have the ability to sustain us through life's challenges.

---

38   Ann and Barry Ulanov, *Religion and the Unconscious* (Philadelphia: The Westminster Press, 1975), p. 144.

39   *Ibid.*, p. 143.

Part II

ॐ

Ethics in Analysis

CHAPTER 6

Integrity of Analysis: Boundaries

Every person in analysis is engaged at a level of core vulnerability. It is not too great a leap, then, to assert that every therapist at every moment with every patient has a duty to protect the core vulnerability of the patient.

—Peter Rutter[1]

In Part I, Individuation as an Ethical Process, we explored the various philosophical and mythological aspects of ethics, morality, and conscience, and saw how Jung understood them to be fundamental to the individuation process. Like the Ancient Greeks and the German philosophers of the nineteenth century, Jung was convinced that when a person was confronted by the unconscious, he needed to rely on the strength and courage of his ego. We appreciate this perspective all the more by reading about Jung's own experience of the unconscious and his struggle to re-create and connect to the divine source within. Jung experienced this divine source as different from the prescribed collective definition of divinity advocated by his family—particularly by his father—and then later by Freud. Our understanding of analytical psychology is thus linked with our knowledge of Jung's personal psychology. Following in Jung's footsteps, we have also come to understand that the individuation journey springs partly from the need to separate from the collective, in order to find our own integrity, moral stance, authenticity, and individual "Voice of God."[2]

---

1   Peter Rutter, "Ethics in Analysis," in The *Transcendent Function: Individual and Collective Aspects: Proceedings of the 12th International IAAP Congress, Chicago, 1992* (Eisendlen: Daimon Verlag, 1993), p. 490.

2   As was discussed in Chapter 2, the "Voice of God" is defined an individual's experience of subjective truth and the divine within.

We exist in a world which unconsciously follows a morality that is not linked to a religious framework that would give the ethical conversation some kind of a moral compass. Consequently, the human species relies on its own definition of what is moral and/or ethical. As a result, an "anything goes" philosophy has arisen. Such a philosophy supports "doing your own thing" and encourages expressions of morality that do not necessarily arise from a conscious struggle or from one's own character but from personal opinion and narcissism. This attitude can be inadvertently adopted because of the duality within the archetype of the Child. On the one hand, the Child is the innermost ethical core of the personality, the bearer of the Self, and the carrier of the personality's wholeness, integrity, and authenticity. On the other hand, the Child is also the carrier of the undeveloped parts of our personality that challenge our integrity. The psychological orphan, with its distancing from collective expectations, is also an aspect of the archetype of the Child. Because the Child carries the parts of personality that undeveloped, infantile and repressed, destructive behaviour/attitudes are also characteristic of the psychological orphan. When analysts tap into these negative aspects, they can fall dangerously close to the Shadow side of Jung's legacy and imitate his own unethical behaviour toward some of his clients. In her presentation at the 1992 IAAP Congress in Chicago,[3] Beverly Zabriske pointed out:

> More than any other, then, the archetype of the orphan has shaped the collective Jungian psyche. The freedom to be oneself is the birthright of the psychological orphan: allowing for originality and the initiative of one without accepted origins, not initiated into any tribe. In its positive aspect psychological orphanhood creates psychic soil for the inspired and individual stance, unbound by collective convention .... But in its negative form, exclusion breeds a defensive belief in one's own specialness, the birthright claimed as entitlement, so often the companion to nursed injury, by which one believes oneself granted right and privilege beyond the given to make for the never received or too soon lost. If not understood and soothed, inflation and corrosive envy breed contempt and spawn disdain for more settled—and more restricted—mortals and their mores. The uncontained may claim not to be accountable and the orphan becomes the renegade, answerable only to needs, drives and appetites .... The entitlement is an especially treacherous underside in those who claim to help and to guide.

---

3   Beverley Zabriske, "Ethics in Analysis," in *The Transcendent Function*, p. 509.

In analytic practice, the psychologically orphaned may disdain professional tenets of practice and ethics.

Every day, Jungian analysts experience tension in their practices between individuation and responsibility to the collective. As a result, examination of this phenomenon has dominated much of the Jungian literature on the collective application of ethics, as analysts struggle with respecting the individual psyche's voice in a collective that largely ignores it. Analytical psychology has come increasingly under pressure from government regulation, insurance company requirements, and expectations of clients for immediate and quick solutions to their problems. First seen in the United States, this pressure has moved to the United Kingdom, Germany, Canada, and Switzerland, and psychotherapists are now regulated professionals in many countries. This increase in rules and regulations also correlates to the rise of feminism and sociopolitical movements that have pushed society to address various types of abuse and psychological trauma. Political activists raised awareness of the damaging effects of abuse, including abuse of therapists and analysts, challenged the prevailing norm of blaming the victim, and forced the collective to respond through legislation. Now, forty years later, our society is dominated by the archetype of the Victim with its propensity to blame others, to seek redress through the courts, and to avoid responsibility for the aspects of one's own destiny that can be controlled. The psychology of the Victim fuels the need for professional liability insurance and restricts genuine emotional responses from analysts, as they fear malpractice allegations and civil law suits.

Part II, Ethics in Analysis, looks at current issues related to practising analytical psychology in the context of the collective. It focuses on analytic boundaries as they support or violate the integrity of the analysand, the analytic container, the work, and the analyst. I argue that analytic boundaries are not rigid constructs. However, this raises the question of how rigid or flexible they should be and how analysands experience them. In this chapter, we will consider the archetypal underpinnings of the analytic relationship, which support the need for boundaries to protect the sacred *temenos* of the container. Does the setting have the greatest influence on defining the container or does the attitude of the analyst make a greater contribution to holding the psychotherapeutic process? Within the context of the analytic relationship, the analytic frame can be made flexible to some extent, as a reflection of genuine human compassion and concern for the Other. In the realm of the Heart and the ethics of integrity and authenticity, the strength of Eros between analyst and analysand can tolerate flexibility.

The next chapter (Chapter 7) examines boundary violations and the Shadow of the profession . We look at the early history of boundary violations and their common features, and decide whether there can be a distinction between an honest mistake and a violation. Central to this discussion is the degree to which analysts act with integrity if a mistake or violation occurs, and the extent to which they have the ability to ethically confront the Shadow. The personal Shadow of the analyst and the archetypal Shadow of the Healer appear through the emotions of human need such as fear, desire, love, hunger, or fatigue that test analysts every day in practice.

Analytic Boundaries and Maintaining Integrity in Analysis

According to the dictionary definition, a boundary is a limiting line or thing—a border. Beyond that line, some activity or function should not take place. This means that the function of a boundary is to define, to demarcate one thing from another. It also operates as a container of something: geographically, boundaries define the territorial limits of nations; in psychology, the term "ego boundaries" is often used to show the awareness of separateness of the Self from non-Self or others. As in the case of ethics, the idea of the boundary defines our relationship to others and to objects in the external world. There is also a connection between integrity and the concept of the analytic boundary. If individuation as an ethical process promotes integrity, the incarnation of the Self, and furthers the authenticity of the analysand, then one must recognize the connection between the idea of integrity and analytic boundaries. In our earlier discussion of integrity, we looked at a definition that encompassed both wholeness and the ability to be responsible for one's own life, actions, and behaviour. It is as if the integrity of something—in the sense of something unbroken, complete, or whole—is established by boundaries that demarcate its wholeness from another wholeness. Boundaries validate one's uniqueness and individuality as distinct from those of another. Psychologically, the experience of being grounded in one's own integrity also implies the psychological experience of knowing one's own boundaries.

Both Jung and his analysands had experiences of the unconscious that informed Jung's theories of analytical psychology. Psychological insight into the world of the unconscious can be confirmed and supported only by the "sincere and honest testimony of other seekers. Our only proof is our experience and [that of] others, since psychic reality cannot be grasped statistically or causally in the sense of the natural sciences."[4] This implies that the role of the analyst is to support the client's subjective experience of the unconscious and thereby help her work toward greater wholeness, that is, *integrity*. The analyst's own ethical confrontation with the unconscious better equips her to support and guide the client's experience and thus cultivate her client's integrity, as well as her own. Boundaries within the analytic situation are therefore needed to facilitate integrity.

In the analytic literature, the discussion of boundaries has focused largely on defining optimal conditions for the work. Analytic boundaries, for instance, are defined as time and place of meeting, the fee to be paid and when, the length of the session, confidentiality, and contact made outside sessions. They are communicated from analyst to analysand through explicit, articulated expectations and agreement, but also through nonverbal messages given through the analyst's behaviour. More than what is said, the way an analyst behaves reflects his personal and professional ego boundaries, his attitudes toward the work and the setting, and his personal values. It is also in the analyst's behaviour that the Shadow can manifest itself in a way that is contrary to the ego's stated intentions.

Analytic boundaries provide the frame, or as Winnicott suggests, the "holding environment" for both analysand and analyst. It allows for the client's expressions of fantasy and symbol, offers the safety to enter into a personal regression, and provides a space for transference and countertransference fantasies to emerge. Glen Gabbard and Eva Lester point out that "Boundaries define the parameters of the analytic relationship so that both patient and analyst can be safe while also being spontaneous."[5] These boundaries also provide the proper container for the activation of affect and instinct, which is necessary for deep analysis. The container provides a place of understanding and symbolization, rather than just a place for acting out of unconscious material.

It would be easy to interpret analytic boundaries as an arbitrary set of rules that reflect an attitude that is rigid, remote, and lacking in feeling. However, a healthy analytic frame, like a healthy ego, is dynamic and flexible. Flexibility allows for dialogue with the environment and accommodates the growth needs of the client as they evolve through the work. Therefore,

---

4   Adolf Guggenbühl-Craig, *Power in the Helping Professions* (Woodstock, CT: Spring Publications, 1971), p. 27.

5   Glen Gabbard and Eva Lester, *Boundaries and Boundary Violations in Psychoanalysis* (New York: Basic Books Inc., 1995), p. 41.

analytic boundaries must be permeable at the same time as providing a container.[6]

Jung's symbol for the analytic space came from his work in alchemy. The images of the "spell-binding circle," the "sacred *temenos*," and the *vas bene clausum*, which Jung equates with the analytic container, allude to the need "to protect what is within from the intrusion and admixture of what is without, as well as to prevent it from escaping."[7] These images have their origins in holy and inviolable places, which reinforces the sacred covenant implicit in the analytic work. The *temenos* was originally a piece of land or a garden dedicated to God and under the auspices of the church. Similarly, Jung's metaphors of the analytic vessel provide a model where the base aspects of the personality can be brought to consciousness and transformed, and where the Self can incarnate. The alchemists' hermetically sealed vessel is connected with Hermes/Mercurius—the spirit of the unconscious. Mercurius is needed to activate the unconscious, but he is also a duplicitous and unstable spirit. In his duplicity, he can be either a healer or a destroyer, and he needs to be contained within the feminine vessel. This links to the feminine principle of Eros and to Carol Gilligan's notion of an "Ethic of Care," which depends on values of responsibility and relationship that make the analysand's psychological development paramount. The closed container is vitally important to the development of the ego, and this development is needed before the ego can incarnate the Self. Leakage contaminates the process and is ultimately a violation of the Self—or the core personality—that is trying to become incarnate.

Archetypal Basis of the Analytic Relationship

The analytic relationship has an archetypal core that informs our innate understanding of the healer-patient dyad, our expectations, and our emotional responses when these expectations are not met. This underlying archetype determines the way the client perceives and evaluates the analyst, and moves the relationship beyond an ordinary business agreement to the level of a covenant, or sacred promise, with all that this implies in terms of moral behaviour. If the archetypal nature of the analytic relationship is not understood or not recognized, there is the danger that it can be acted out unconsciously in a sexual relationship or through other, non-sexual boundary violations.

---

6   Richard S. Epstein, *Keeping Boundaries: Maintaining Safety and Integrity in the Psychotherapeutic Process* (Washington: American Psychiatric Press, Inc., 1994), p. 17.

7   C.G. Jung, *Psychology and Alchemy*, Vol. 12 of *The Collected Works* (Princeton, NJ: Princeton University Press, 1968), paragraph 219.

At the archetypal core of the occupation of the analyst are the images of the Divine Healer, the Priest, and the Shaman—metaphors Jung used himself when describing the analytic work. These provide the archetypal underpinnings of the analytic relationship and precursors for the trust and faith the client places in the analyst. The archetypal dynamic is also present in any professional relationship in which we place faith and trust in another to preserve, protect, and treat our minds, bodies, or souls. Society has traditionally anointed certain professionals—such as lawyers, clergy, doctors, teachers, and analysts—with special status because of their ability to take care of specific human needs. By conferring this status, we place great value on meeting those needs, and we assume that these individuals are models of wisdom and morality.[8] In placing faith in the professional, we also naturally relinquish a certain amount of power.

The Shaman, in primitive societies, was a magician, medicine man, doctor, and healer, who played an essential role in maintaining the psychological integrity of the community. His or her function was to attend to the physical, emotional, social, and spiritual needs of community members, and to defend against disease, death, sterility, disaster, and the world of darkness. Ultimate faith was placed in the Shaman's abilities to call upon the positive forces of the spiritual world. The contemporary equivalent to this kind of healer has a similarly exalted status, and this informs a client's response when flexibility of boundaries leads to healing or when abuse of power and boundary violations lead to wounding and traumatization.

In discussing the transference and countertransference dynamics between analyst and analysand, Jung based many of his comments on a Shamanistic model of healing as the archetypal foundation for depth analysis. Much like the Shaman, the analyst takes over the sufferings of his patient as a way to fashion a cure. In her article "Profession and Vocation," Marie-Louise von Franz suggests that the helper of the psyche or the soul is the person who can heal himself or herself and is therefore in a position to help others. "Such a person," she writes, "is intact in his innermost core and possesses ego strength, two indispensable prerequisites for the profession of therapist. He undergoes his initiatory illness not out of weakness, but rather in order to become acquainted with all the ways of sickness to know from his own experience what possession, depression, schizoid dissociation and so on mean."[9]

---

8   Marilyn Peterson, *At Personal Risk: Boundary Violations in Professional-Client Relationships* (New York: W.W. Norton & Company, 1992), p. 11.

9   Marie-Louise von Franz, "Profession and Vocation" in *Psychotherapy* (Boston: Shambhala Publications), pp. 277–278.

In its ideal form, the client experiences analysis as an active process of self-healing within the context of the relationship with the analyst. It is the encounter with the analyst that evokes the archetype of the Divine Healer, and the transpersonal or archetypal dimensions of the psyche within the client. Edward Whitmont describes this dynamic in *The Alchemy of Healing*: "The concept and symbolic image of the divine healer expresses a particular field dynamic, personal and transpersonal, that arises between healer and patient by virtue of their mutual encounter."[10]

We can see the parallel between the Shamanistic model of the analytic relationship and Jung's image that there is a quarternity within any human relationship, as he explains in *The Psychology of Transference*.[11] This quarternity comes from the alchemical *quarternio* of sacred marriage and reflects the six lines of crossing energy between any two people in relationship. In *The Analytic Encounter: Transference and Human Relationship*,[12] Mario Jacoby extends the model so that it applies to the transference between analyst and client in any gender configuration. The arrows in the diagram show the various lines of communication that exist between analyst and analysand, including those between (a) the egos of the analyst and the analysand; (b) the unconscious of the analyst and the unconscious of the analysand; c) the analyst's ego and her own unconscious; (d) the client's ego and her unconscious; (e) the analyst's ego and the client's unconscious; and (f) the client's ego and the analyst's unconscious.

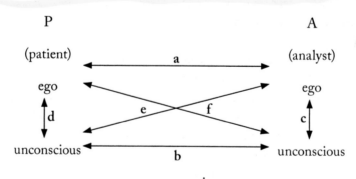

P   A

(patient)   a   (analyst)

ego   ego

d   e   f   c

unconscious   b   unconscious

common unconsciousness

---

10   Edward Whitmont, *The Alchemy of Healing* (Berkeley, CA: North Atlantic Books, 1993), p. 188.

11   C.G. Jung, "The Psychology of the Transference" in *The Practice of Psychotherapy*, Vol. 16 of *The Collected Works* (Princeton, NJ: Princeton University Press, 1966).

12   Mario Jacoby, *The Analytic Encounter: Transference and Human Relationship* (Toronto: Inner City Books, 1984).

The arrows emanating from the unconscious of one partner to the unconscious of the other represent projections. This is as true for the analyst as it is for the analysand, which is why Jung believed that every analyst should have completed analysis in order to increase his awareness of his own inner dynamics, complexes, and weaknesses. This model illustrates that the analytic work exists at many different levels and reflects the notion that an energetic field exists between analyst and the analysand. It also illustrates the fact that the analyst can be drawn into pitfalls by projecting unconscious material onto the client, or because a comment from a client touches a particularly sensitive spot in the analyst's psyche, or because the analyst's and client's wounds are similar.

When there is a striking resemblance between the analyst's countertransference and the client's wound, the Shamanistic model can be seen. The analyst becomes infected with the analysand's illness through the interactive field and works through that illness by analyzing the inner psychological constellation the sickness creates. By working through the constellation— expressed in dreams, associations, and other unconscious material—the analyst is able to heal herself through symbols. Then she fashions the "medicine" within herself and administers it to the analysand via her "influence" within the analytic field. Out of her own personal need for healing, the analyst is forced to develop further by dealing with the effects created by the analysand's illness.[13] Therefore, in depth analysis, the Shamanistic healing process is conducted on the psychic plane, rather than the physical plane, and the analyst offers herself as medicine through the process of being in touch with and integrating her own wound within herself.

The symbol of the Shaman is also part of the archetype of the Wise Old Man/Wise Old Woman. In this archetype rests the *"mana"* personality, the superior master and teacher inherent in the role of guru, magician, doctor, or any person who possesses authority and who carries the potential for healing and meaning amidst the chaos of life. As an image from the collective unconscious, the Shaman is a particularly gifted personality endowed with magic power, often personified as the mighty wise person, the hero or heroine, the chief, the magician, the medicine woman, and/or the friend of God.

As a result of this archetypal underpinning, the client is encouraged to behave toward the analyst in a certain way. For example, the client is taught that his cooperation is necessary to obtain the maximum benefit from the analyst's expertise and knowledge, that he should comply with the analyst's

---

13   Murray Stein, "Power, Shamanism, and Maieutics in the Countertransference," in *Transference Countertransference* (Wilmette, IL: Chiron Publications, 1984), p. 78.

directives, and that his needs will be placed ahead of the analyst's needs. As such, the nature of the relationship between the analyst and the analysand is raised "to the level of a covenant of professional promise and personal trust,"[14] according to which the client is required to put faith in unknown abilities. At this level, the relationship between client and professional takes on a spiritual quality. The ancient Greeks were also aware of this level of the doctor-patient relationship, as the Hippocratic Oath was framed in the context of allegiance to the gods.

By its archetypal nature, the analytic relationship places the analysand in a psychologically vulnerable position: he turns to a stranger for assistance—a stranger who has been granted status by the collective through specific training, expertise, and knowledge. The client's need and his unstated and invisible faith in the ability of the analyst to respond or to help in a time of crisis contribute to the analysand's tendency to hand over a degree of control and power. *It is the handing over of control and power that emphasizes the client's vulnerability and diminishes his ability to be self-determining and to question the work of the analyst.*[15]

The relationship between analyst and analysand is not a mutual or equal one, and the power imbalance intensifies during the work. In his article, "Is the Analytical Situation Shame-producing?"[16] Mario Jacoby suggests that the inequality of the analytic situation has the potential to produce shame and humiliation in the analysand. The client comes to the analyst to address certain needs in his life that he is unable to address or resolve on his own. He therefore has the expectation that the analyst will heal his suffering, have the right answers, or know what to do in a particular crisis situation. The degree of crisis or the depth of neediness may also contribute to the analysand's tendency to give over power to the analyst. This power imbalance is reinforced throughout the work, as the analysand reveals the most intimate details of his life—including possibly embarrassing fantasies and feelings about the analyst—while knowing nothing about the personal life of the analyst.

In many cases, a resolution of the initial crisis that brought the client into analysis is not immediately forthcoming, and the analysand is required to wait

---

14   Peterson, *At Personal Risk*, p. 12.

15   This is a critical product of the analytic situation because many clients confronted with boundary violations have pointed out that they were unable to question the analyst when violations first occurred.

16   Mario Jacoby, "Is the Analytic Situation Shame-Producing?", *Journal of Analytical Psychology 38* (1993), pp. 419–435.

for something to emerge. This waiting furthers his dependency and vulnerability. In addition, if an aspect of analysis is the incarnation of the Self in the analysand, the analysand's first experience of this can be numinous. If there is no place else for the new sense of Self to go, it will be projected onto the analyst, who then carries the image of the Self or God for the client. This situation further contributes to the client's loss of judgement and surrendering of individual power. The analyst can then be tempted to identify with the projection of the Self or the archetype of the Healer and assume power that she does not have.

Marilyn Peterson suggests that the power in the analytic situation originates mostly from outside the situation—societal ascription, expert knowledge, and clients' expectations and projections. Other factors contributing to the sense of power surrounding the analyst include the analyst's own relationship to authority figures in her childhood, feelings of self-worth and entitlement, the way she defines herself as an authority figure within the analytic frame, and the way she uses that authority in relationship to clients. The analyst has a greater knowledge base from which to draw, exercises power in terms that define the setting in which sessions take place, and determines the boundaries of access through other forms of contact, such as telephone conversations. While the analyst creates an atmosphere of neutrality in order to help the analytic process, the work by its very nature produces anxiety, shame, dependency, and vulnerability in the client, and this recreates the dependency inherent in the parent-child dynamic of childhood.

Analytic Boundaries: Flexibility or Violation?

In both the psychoanalytic and the Jungian literature, there is a general consensus that analytic boundaries should be permeable and flexible—not rigid or static structures. The description suggests a flow, a back-and-forth between analyst and analysand. If there is a strict and rigid adherence to the analytic frame on the one hand and a total disregard for boundaries on the other, there exists a "grey" area where mutuality, Eros, and basic humanity exist. According to a strict Freudian view, neutrality and detachment are believed to be essential to the work. They promote transference by allowing the analysand to project onto the analyst whatever needs to be brought to consciousness. However, by taking this approach too far, the analyst can become excessively remote and distant. At the other end of the spectrum, analysts who allow their own material to interfere with the client's treatment contaminate the client's natural process. As psychologist Melvin Miller puts it, "If therapists never allow themselves to be drawn into participation with patients in their enactments, then we speak of a failure of empathy. On the other hand, if therapists allow themselves to be drawn into their patient's internal dramas but they get lost in the re-enactment, then we speak of a failure of containment."[17]

Jung was a pioneer in emphasizing that the analyst's genuine and authentic emotional involvement was essential to the analytic process. Using the image of mixing chemical substances, both analyst and analysand are in the analytic work together, and it is within this relationship that consciousness takes place. Martin Buber's I-Thou relational perspective suggests that "relationship is the medium through which the human being grows, develops and matures, and it is the vehicle through which the sense of self gradually unfolds."[18] Such a relationship perspective requires a specific attitude of relating to the "genuine otherness of the other person. Meaning that I in my own totality am relating to Thou in his or her own totality."[19] This perspective correlates to Erikson's mature adult ethical orientation, which rests in mutuality and responsibility.

In the grey area of collective ethical codes and the feelings between two individuals in an analytic process, the issue of flexibility and Eros is a delicate and precarious concern. Alterations to the container can constitute a "detrimental acting out" by the analyst, done under the pretext of humanness and flexibility, or they can be extremely beneficial to the client's process and healing. In a lecture entitled "Erotic Transference and Countertransference: Issues of Ethics and Soul," Jungian analyst Nancy Qualls-Corbett has articulated the dilemma cogently: "And when the soul's need cries out for the warmth of human touch, is it appropriate? The line is very fine indeed. Does one listen to the doctrine or law constructed by external reason and rationality or does one listen to inward ethical guidelines when attending the matters of the soul?"[20]

Following are several examples of cases where analysts have gone outside the analytic frame. Each reflects actions that resulted from the therapists listening to inward ethical guidelines, checking them carefully with accepted professional standards, and making the boundaries of analysis more flexible than usual. Nancy Qualls-Corbett, concerning one of her own difficult clients, describes how the simple gesture of lifting the client's ponytail while helping

---

17   Melvin Miller, "The Mutual Influence and Involvement of Therapist and Patient: Co-contributors to Maturation and Integrity" in *The Psychology of Mature Spirituality* (London: Routledge, 2000), p. 42.

18   *Ibid.*, p. 43.

19   Mario Jacoby, *The Analytic Encounter*, p. 63.

20   Nancy Qualls-Corbett, "Erotic Transference and Countertransference: Issues of Ethics and Soul"(http://www.cgjungpage.org/index2.php?option=com_content&do_pdf=1&id=120).

her put on her coat became a closing ritual that signalled some movement in the analysis and that eventually ended the client's self-destructive behaviour. The gesture had first come from Qualls-Corbett's relationship to her own daughters, and she had instinctively repeated it with her client.

In another case, related by an analysand, a woman was unexpectedly admitted to hospital for a serious operation. The circumstances and suddenness of the procedure meant that she had told no one about it and consequently was prepared to go through the operation alone, without any emotional support. Her relationship with her analyst was relatively formal, and until the time of her operation, involved conventional analytic boundaries and frames. As a result, she did not expect to have contact with her analyst during her convalescence.

However, when she woke up in the recovery room, the first thing she saw was a huge bouquet of flowers and her analyst standing there. Had the analyst not been there, the woman would have woken up from the anaesthesia alone. With the client's permission, the analyst visited her in the hospital every day during her stay. As the analyst recounts the story, it is clear that the beneficial effect of this gesture were profound She wondered if there might not be other contexts in which the analytic frame could be expanded, as long as those alterations were made out of integrity and respect for the client. And she felt that certain aspects of the analytic relationship could not be prescribed by ethical code but must remain within the realm of being human.

In commenting on a similar situation, the authors of "Drawing Boundaries"[21] highlight the need for careful deliberation and the necessity of creating space for both therapist and client to reflect on the experience afterwards. They write:

> What seems most important in this case is that John [the therapist] was not cavalier about his behaviour. He carefully thought out the decision to visit, was deliberate in his actions while at Gina's bedside [the client] and later created a safe forum in which she could discuss the visit's meaning with him. He did not make the mistake of thinking that his visit was equivalent to that of another friend; this was a professional visit that would have symbolic resonance.[22]

---

21 Deborah A. Lott and John Ritter, "Drawing Boundaries," *Psychology Today*, 1 June 1999, pp. 48–52, 76.

22 *Ibid.*, p. 51.

The following story reveals a different set of issues, faced by an analyst struggling with the request of an analysand, who was moving to another city, to go for a walk as their last session. The male analyst describes the analysis as very difficult because the analysand, a young woman, had an intense love transference. As a result of the transference, the client repeatedly requested personal information from the analyst that the analyst experienced as slightly manipulative and intrusive. The client also bitterly complained that the analytic frame was hurtful to her and that she wasn't getting what she needed, accusing the analyst of being self-serving and putting up a wall in order to avoid revealing anything personal. Because of her own story, the analysand felt extremely restricted by collective expectations and norms that appeared to be replicated in the circumstances of the analysis. Although the analysand would not allow herself to voice any fantasies or other symbolic material, she struggled with what was allowed and not allowed in the analysis and in her relationship to the analyst.

The analyst made the decision to agree to the analysand's request, fearing that maintaining a normative idea of what constituted the analytic setting would likely have resulted in a repeat wounding. During the process of deliberation, the analyst reflected a great deal on what constitutes the analytic frame. Was it determined by the time and space of the analytic hour or by the attitude of the analyst, who would contain the process, regardless of the setting? Assistance from his supervisor helped the therapist clarify his authentic feelings about the decision. This meant he could take the walk with the client while maintaining his analytic attitude and containing the analytic process. Because the analyst and the client took the walk, the client felt less wounded by the analytic frame and the analysis ended favourably. In a similar case, London analyst Vernon Yorke[23] describes a woman who, after years of "stuck" analysis, benefited from their session going over the fifty-minute time limit. The analysand, who as a child experienced decisions by her parents as arbitrary and thus having no meaning, also experienced the analytic setting as arbitrary, fixed, and a barrier to projecting material onto the analyst. The analyst describes her as "a person with very rigid barriers, who could not be penetrated" at first, but breakthroughs were made after she experienced the analyst's flexibility.

---

23   Vernon Yorke, "Boundaries, Psychic Structure and Time," *Journal of Analytical Psychology* No. 38 (1993), p. 61.

ða.

In deciding whether more flexible analytic boundaries are appropriate, consideration must be given as to whether the action will serve the client's therapeutic interests and help him on his individuation journey. If any act or encounter threatens that goal, it is suspect, even if its exploitive potential is not obvious. The cases presented here illustrate situations where the analyst's motivations were compassion, humanity, and altruism, which reflected a genuine interest in the client and the client's well-being. While the analysts' actions went beyond the analytic setting, they were still within the context of the analytic relationship and reflected, at least on the surface, qualities of authenticity, genuine concern, and a synthesis of Logos and Eros. These are elements found in Mencius' notion of the Heart-Mind and in the Hindu *Anahata chakra*, which embody the ethics of integrity, authenticity, and compassion. Crucial to making analytic boundaries more flexible is the ethical attitude of the analyst—that is, the integrity she brings to the decision and her willingness to accept responsibility for any mistakes. As part of this willingness, the therapist needs to let the analysand express her reactions to the therapist's actions, and the therapist must also confront her Shadow if her interventions outside the frame do not have the intended results.

CHAPTER 7

The Analyst's Shadow and Boundary Violations

Accepting one's shadow is difficult for one's morality because consciousness must take the unconscious into account.

—Denyse Zemor[1]

The Analyst's Shadow

The *Tai Chi* symbol is one of the best images for Jung's conception of the psyche. It poignantly expresses his ideas of the principle of opposition, and shows
that the totality of the psyche contains both poles—positive and negative, light
and dark, masculine and feminine. Every archetype has positive and negative
expressions. Therefore, in the analytic process, violation is as likely to happen
as healing. Wounding, being wounded, and healing are functional aspects of
the same archetypal pattern of the Wounded Healer. The champion of light
and consciousness can also be the champion of darkness and unconsciousness.
The Holy Man is also the False Prophet. The Child in search of its birthright is
also the renegade Orphan who refuses to follow collective convention.

One of Jung's major insights into the nature of the psyche was this: when
we increase consciousness, we also deepen the Shadow—that is, the part of
us that is unconscious. Behind the idealized figure of the Healer God, there

---

1   Denyse Zemor, "Ethics in Analysis," in *The Transcendent Function: Individual and
     Collective Aspects, Proceedings of the 12th International IAAP Congress, Chicago, 1992*
     (Eisendlen: Daimon Verlag, 1993), p. 494.

lurks the potential invader, attacker, and destroyer, the *diabolos confuser* and the devil.[2] The analyst can poison and add to the patient's disturbance through his Shadow, by acting unconsciously out of his own complexes or out of some emotional need. Analysts' personal needs arising from fear, hunger, desire, fatigue, or the unhealed parts of the psyche test their centredness and integrity, and when the analyst acts out unconsciously from these places, the integrity of the analysis and of the client are compromised. Following the Shamanistic model that was presented in the previous chapter, if the transference and countertransference dynamics become unconscious for the analyst, the analyst's objective view of the client's personality is distorted and merges with the analyst's own Shadow. He then projects inappropriate feelings onto the client, which results in misdiagnosis and misreading of the client's issues. In such a situation, the analyst loses his analytic attitude of keeping the analysand's individuation path paramount.

Adolf Guggenbühl-Craig[3] identifies the analyst's Shadow as the Charlatan and the False Prophet. Marie-Louise von Franz[4] describes this Shadow as the Dark Shaman who practises black magic. Like all archetypes, these figures come from the collective unconscious and strive to oppose the analyst's conscious goals. Power—the opposite of Eros—drives the analyst's charlatan Shadow. In this power dynamic, the use of his healing knowledge is directed toward personal advantage, influence, or financial gain. It is a great temptation for the analyst to abuse his power position, and he can be seduced away from his primary allegiance to the analysand's therapeutic process and ability to look inward. Well-meaning analysts can easily and inadvertently activate the Shadow aspect of the Healer and abuse power in the attempt to relieve the suffering of analysands. They may do this from a desire to be helpful or by acting out what the client missed as a child.

Every analyst is susceptible to the seductive quality of the unconscious, and to being possessed by some unconscious content. At an archetypal level, possession by the Healer archetype is a subtle inflation caused by the ego appropriating something that does not belong to it. Like the Greek idea of hubris, the charlatan Shadow of the professional emerges whenever the ana-

---

2   Edward Whitmont, *The Alchemy of Healing* (New York: North Atlantic Books, 1993), p. 190.

3   Adolf Guggenbühl-Craig, *Power in the Helping Professions* (Woodstock, CT: Spring Publications, 1971).

4   Marie-Louise von Franz, "Profession and Vocation" in *Psychotherapy* (Boston: Shambhala, 1993).

lyst oversteps the boundaries of her abilities or competence, when she fails to recognize human limits. This is a test of the ability to accept such limitations—that is, the capacity to accept the confines of Polly Young-Eisendrath's definition of integrity. The inappropriate crossing of a boundary can be either a relatively minor mistake or a violation, depending on the analyst's ability to confront her own Shadow ethically. John Beebe writes: "If the psyche is to ground itself in a sense of its own reality and the fact of its boundaries, therapists have to do something to acknowledge when they transgress those boundaries, and to atone for the violation of them. Like the real body, the subtle body of the psyche demands respect for its limits —and all hell breaks out when they are not respected."[5] According to this sentiment, it is important for analysts to be involved in an ongoing process of self-examination and to accept responsibility for their own unconsciousness, in order to support clients in their own confrontations with painful insights and with the Shadow.

Boundary Violations and Ethics in Analysis

Psychoanalysts and others have written extensively about analysts acting out sexually. There is general agreement that this is clearly unethical behaviour and damaging to the client. However, boundary violations also include much subtler dilemmas with social, financial, and narcissistic features, and in many cases, non-sexual boundary violations represent the beginning of the slippery slope toward more serious sexual violations. At their worst, these transgressions can be equally damaging.

In the previous chapter, I suggested that analytic boundaries are defined as much by the analytic frame as they are by the analyst's ego boundaries. Working with the unconscious in a depth analysis poses a constant danger of losing ego boundaries. At an archetypal level, identification with the Healer or other god-image is a major inflation and hubris of the will, whereby the individual appropriates a power that he does not own. From her study of fairy tales, Marie-Louise von Franz suggests that a number of common factors come into play when people fall under the spell of some possession,[6] that is, when they clinically lose their ego boundaries in a confrontation with the unconscious. Von Franz writes: "If you look at the conditions under which people fall into

---

5   John Beebe, *Integrity in Depth* (New York: From International Publishing, 1995), pp. 19–20.

6   Marie-Louise von Franz, *Shadow and Evil in Fairy Tales* (Boston: Shambhala Publications, 1995), p. 172.

evil, you will see certain features which are common to practically all the stories. In several, drinking played a role in some form or another, so drinking is for the primitive one of the simplest and easiest ways by which he opens the door to being possessed by evil. Another is loneliness, being alone, being separated from the village group or the tribal group to which he belongs."

The Renegade Orphan Shadow of the Divine Child removes himself from collective rules. While separation from the collective is a necessary step in the path of individuation, von Franz clearly articulates the danger of falling into the negative side of the unconscious because of this isolation. From this standpoint, analysts who have somehow become separated from the collective professional analytic community might be in particular danger of falling prey to such inflation.

Robert Epstein offers a more clinical explanation:

> Boundary violations are most likely to occur when the therapist's ego boundaries have been disrupted in some way. For instance, a therapist's ego boundaries may be chronically defective because of a mental disorder such as sociopathology, psychosis, neurotic conflict, pathological narcissism, or dementia. An acute break of ego boundaries can be triggered by general factors in the therapist's life or by the specific stress of dealing with an individual patient.[7]

Epstein goes on to identify three stages related to the erosion of therapeutic boundaries, associated with functions of the analyst.

> 1. The therapist suffers from an acute or chronic dysregulation of his or her ego boundaries. The impairment may consist of overly porous boundaries, overly 'thick' boundaries, or a combination of the two.

Many causes could be related to this. The analyst might have insufficient knowledge of the nature and function of therapeutic boundaries, or could suffer from a disruption in his or her personal life or some mental disorder that results in an ego impairment of some kind.

> 2. The therapist employs maladaptive intrapsychic methods in an attempt to compensate for the impaired boundary functioning.

---

7   Robert Epstein, *Keeping Boundaries: Maintaining Safety and Integrity in the Psychotherapeutic Process* (Washington, D.C.: American Psychiatric Press, 1994), p. 91.

For example, narcissistic or grandiose defences that deny the client's needs for boundaries and based on the analyst's failure to recognize the boundary violations. Usually this mechanism is used to avoid feelings of shame and vulnerability. It can be a way of preserving a self-image of professional competence and mental stability. It asserts "I cannot bear to see myself as imperfect, therefore I needn't ask for help from another professional."

> 3. The therapist uses non-therapeutic behaviour ... in order to compensate for the impaired boundary functioning.[8]

For example, to avoid experiencing the aggression, accusations, or feelings of professional incompetence, the therapist acts out unconsciously. The acting out by the analyst serves primarily to avoid his or her own internal disharmony.

Early History of Boundary Violations

According to Glen Gabbard and Eva Lester, the notion of analytic boundaries has appeared relatively recently in the psychoanalytic and Jungian literature. In *Boundaries and Boundary Violations in Psychoanalysis*, their investigation of the early years of psychoanalysis, they point out that the pioneers in Freud's circle were, in fact, experimenting with the complexity of transference and countertransference dynamics, and in the process found themselves "sucked into the vortex of a host of major boundary transgressions."[9] However, the questionable behaviour of early analysts can be understood only partly through this experimentation of trial and error that was part of the birthing process of psychoanalysis. Many knew that some of their actions were inadvisable and tried to keep their activities secret from their colleagues.

The most notable of Jung's transgressions was his relationship with Sabina Spielrein, which began in 1904. She became his first analytic case when she was admitted to the Burghölzli for hysteria, where she was a hospital resident from August, 1904, to May, 1905. She was nineteen years old and Jung was twenty-nine. He had only recently— in 1903—married Emma, and was the newly "anointed" heir-apparent to Freud. As he embarked on his work with Spielrein, he was also launching into his first opportunity to apply the psychoanalytic method. Jung fell victim to enacting an unconscious countertrans-

---

8   *Ibid.*, p. 92.
9   Glen Gabbard and Eva Lester, *Boundaries and Boundary Violations in Psychoanalysis* (New York: Basic Books, 1995), p. 69.

ference that, according to Jungian analyst Greg Mogenson, was associated with Jung's resistance to the methods he was applying.[10] As a result of her own resistance to Jung's interpretations of her condition, Spielrein developed a transference neurosis that manifested in the form of "Siegfried," the incestuous imaginary love child that was the product of their union.

Following termination of the treatment, Sabine left the hospital to study medicine, and she and Jung developed a working relationship that soon intensified into a friendship. Despite Sabina's discharge from hospital, the transference-countertransference dynamics that existed in the analytic relationship persisted long afterwards. Four years after the initial analysis, the two became friends and Spielrein claimed that they were lovers. When Jung attempted to end the relationship, Spielrein attacked him, an action that reflects the degree to which she felt betrayed by him. In descriptions of the relationship by John Kerr[11] and Jungian analyst Aldo Carotenuto[12], a common image emerges— that of an archetypal bond between Jung and Spielrein. Each believed that the other was a soul mate and that some mystical or telepathic connection existed between them. Based on his in-depth exploration of their writings during this time, John Kerr suggests that elements of death and destruction were prominent themes for both of them, especially in connection with sexuality. This may have contributed to the attraction. Greg Mogenson has proposed that the relationship was a means for Jung to break from Freud and to return to his pre-Freudian interests of mythology, parapsychology, astrology, and the occult.

When the affair was over and Spielrein was desperately hurt, Jung attempted to redeem himself in at least two unsolicited letters to her mother. He rationalized his behaviour by claiming that he never charged her a fee for his services, as if that somehow absolved him from his actions and the harm they caused. Research reveals that he took several steps to hide the true nature of the relationship from both Freud and Spielrein's mother by questioning Spielrein's version of events and her mental stability. Her desperation and incoherence helped minimize Jung's embarrassment and appeared to support his claim that she had misunderstood. Shortly afterwards, in 1909, she wrote to Freud, telling him about the affair, but Freud apparently did not take her accu-

---

10   Greg Mogenson, "Barnstock's Progeny: The Sword of Incest and the Tree of Life in Freud, Jung and Spielrein," *Quadrant 2* (2000).

11   John Kerr, *A Most Dangerous Method: The Story of Jung, Freud and Sabina Spielrein* (New York: Knopf, 1993).

12   Aldo Carotenuto, *A Secret Symmetry: Sabina Spielrein between Jung and Freud* (New York: Pantheon Books, 1982).

sations seriously and seemed to accept Jung's explanation that she was emotionally disturbed. As Glen Gabbard and Eva Lester write, "the relationship nearly destroyed Jung's career and brought Spielrein to the edge of despair."[13]

Practising analytical psychologists have inherited the early boundary violations by the founders of psychoanalysis—especially Jung's relationship with Sabina Spielrein and later Toni Wolff. This behaviour was not unique to Jung. Situations that are now considered to be clearly beyond acceptable analytic boundaries can be found among many leaders in the field, including Melanie Klein, Ernest Jones, and Donald Winnicott. Since analysts are unable to rely on the founders as present-day role models for us, there is sometimes lack of clarity and confusion as to what constitutes a boundary violation—especially a non-sexual one. Gabbard and Lester argue that it is very important to look at the history of analytic boundaries, much in the same way it is essential to look at the history of our families. They write:

> In the mid-60s, a training analyst in an institute was charged with sexual misconduct. Two decades later, two analysts he had analysed were also charged with sexual misconduct in the same city. Blind spots in one analytic generation may well become blind spots in the next. Our emphasis on the historical legacy can be problematic, however, if we misuse it to blame our analytic parents rather than address basic challenges of the analytic situation that transcend time and place.[14]

As we will see later, Gabbard raises an extremely important consideration: the ethical attitude of training analysts and supervisors are major contributing factors in the development of an ethical attitude in candidates.

Common Features of Boundary Violations

All boundary violations have similar characteristics and are well described by Professor Marilyn Peterson:

> Boundary violations are acts that breach the core intent of the professional-client association. They happen when professionals exploit the relationship to meet personal needs rather than client needs. Changing that fundamental principle undoes the covenant, altering the ethos of care

---

13   Gabbard and Lester, *Boundaries and Boundary Violations*, p. 73.
14   *Ibid.*, p. 86.

that obliges professionals to place clients' concerns first. In fact, all of the boundaries in a professional client relationship exist in order to protect this core understanding.[15]

In other words, boundary violations disturb the analytic relationship and subvert the original purpose of the relationship by turning it into something else. In her book *At Personal Risk*, Marilyn Peterson outlines the four characteristics that have emerged in every story of sexual and non-sexual boundary violations she has researched: reversal of roles, secrecy, a double bind, and indulgence of professional privilege.

1. Reversal of Roles

The essential feature of this type of violation is that the professional and the client reverse roles so that the analysand/client becomes the caretaker for the analyst. The analyst structures encounters or sessions so that his needs and gratification become the primary focus. The analyst, who rationalizes his behaviour as being for the client's benefit, often creates such a situation unconsciously. The shift in the dynamic of the relationship changes the status of the client by bestowing on him a new power that is experienced as an elevation and a natural high. The analysand feels special, validated, and chosen, but he mistakenly feels that it is about who he is as a person. This special status gives him false validation because he is only considered "special" because of his ability to look after the analyst's needs. "Not knowing the real reason behind the change of status," writes Peterson, "the client follows the professional's lead."[16] Although the client psychologically experiences the redefinition of the relationship as a significant alteration, in reality, he has very little power or control over that change in status.

2. Secrecy

Important information and knowledge are withheld from the client as to the true nature of the analyst's motivations: for example, the analyst may invite a client to an event in the hopes of a sexual liaison or she may terminate a client in order to take advantage of the client's skills for her own business. The result is an erosion of the honesty and integrity of the analytic relationship, a contamination of trust, and harm done to the client's psychological

---

15   Marilyn Peterson, *At Personal Risk: Boundary Violations in Professional–Client Relationships* (New York: W.W. Norton & Company, 1992), p. 75.

16   *Ibid.*, p. 78.

well-being. As Peterson writes: "Without the critical knowledge required for a reasonable choice on the client's part, the client is manipulated into participating unknowingly in the professional's plan."[17] The analyst acts out of a secret motivation or hidden agenda, more than out of regard for her client's needs or therapeutic benefit. Because of the presence of a dual agenda, the client's reality function is seriously damaged. In other words, the dual agenda is "crazy-making," since the analysand is unable to realistically interpret the actions of the analyst.

3. A Double Bind

The actions of the analyst place the analysand in a double bind, where movement in any direction creates a dilemma or is perceived as hazardous. Any decision the client makes is experienced as resulting in some loss, and consequently, she feels unable to overcome the impasse. The client may either betray the analytic relationship by commenting on the violation, or violate her own integrity by continuing to participate in the situation set up by the therapist. In either case, the psychological significance is that the client fails to listen to her own inner voice telling her that something is wrong. She becomes frozen by fear, and falls into unconscious collusion with the analyst in order to avoid facing what is actually happening. Peterson goes on to say:

> Boundary violations place clients in untenable binds. Since they are highly dependent on the professional, clients feel both trapped inside the relationship and bound by their perceived inability to move independently. They are tied both by what they need from the professional and by their fear of being without the relationship. If they give up the relationship, they lose the professional's needed expertise. If they stay in the relationship, they lose a part of their personhood.[18]

The client is especially vulnerable to damage when an analyst working with the client's unconscious places the client in a double bind. As mentioned above, the nature of the analytic work inherently requires analysts to support the client's subjective experience of the unconscious, in order to gain psychological insights into the truth about his life. But by undermining the client's reality function and thereby damaging his psychological well-being, the analyst fails to strengthen the ego in order to meet the unconscious. Instead, there

---

17   Peterson, *At Personal Risk*, p. 81.
18   *Ibid.*, p. 87.

could be dissolution of the ego function. At its worst, such violation could lead to serious psychological consequences, including psychosis.

4. Indulgence of Professional Privilege

In every boundary violation, there is a fit between the professional's need and the client's vulnerability[19] that allows the analyst to take advantage of the client. At one level, violating behaviour could arise from the analyst's sense of entitlement. At another level, a *folie à deux,* or mutual unconsciousness, could arise because the two parties have similar wounds. In either case, the indulgence of personal privilege is propelled by the immediacy of the professional's need and by her motive in the relationship.[20] As the analyst changes the circumstances or the nature of the relationship, she often rationalizes her behaviour as being inconsequential or even helpful for the client. At best, these rationalizations are a function of twisted logic, where the claim of benevolence allows the analyst to hide what is really going on.

Analytic Boundaries: Flexibility or Violation? Three Case Studies

The following case studies highlight the negative of effects of non-sexual boundary violations. Individual therapists and analysts who experienced boundary violations in one of their personal analysis provided the material for the first two cases. They graciously agreed to allow their stories to be told, and the accounts are being included with their editorial assistance. Names have been changed and considerable efforts have been made to alter the description of any circumstances that might identify the actual people in question. The third case is a composite of a number of stories that were presented to me during my research. Unlike the case presentations in the previous chapter, which described incidents where analytic boundaries were made flexible with beneficial effect, these stories highlight situations where the client experienced a violation of the analytic container, with destructive consequences. All display the common features described above: reversal of roles, secrecy, a double bind, and indulgence of professional privilege. The sacred covenant of the analytic relationship was broken when the analyst's personal needs took precedence over the needs of the client and the process. All three clients felt significantly wounded by the transgressions of their analysts, and the situation deteriorated further when the analyst refused to acknowledge that a change had happened, thus leaving the client to bear the consciousness of the violation alone.

---

19 *Ibid.,* p. 90.
20 *Ibid.,* p. 92.

1. The Story of Susan

The first story involves a woman—I will call her Susan—who entered analysis with a senior analyst who also happened to be her first analyst's analyst. Susan's first analyst was a student who had finished her training and was relocating. She referred Susan to her own training analyst after Susan had a dream of him. Susan did not know at the time that the two analysts were in an intimate relationship. As a respected senior analyst who had a notable reputation in the community, Susan's new analyst was viewed with a certain amount of awe, so she looked forward to her meetings with him. She describes the first several months of analysis as helpful. The analyst had a warm quality, which helped Susan address her negative father complex. However, the analyst was often late, and Susan could wait for as long as thirty minutes for her session. Sometimes the analyst would emerge from a session with his previous client, announce that he needed something to drink, and suggest that they move the session to a nearby coffee shop.

The analysis quickly took on a different quality when Susan had a dream of him and her first analyst. Instead of analyzing the dream, the analyst took the opportunity to tell Susan about the relationship he had with her previous analyst. In many sessions, the analyst reversed the nature of the discussion to talk about the difficulties he was experiencing with this woman. He also talked openly about his negative feelings regarding other analysts in the community. The analyst continually warned Susan to "stay away from so and so," and in so doing this created the impression that none of his colleagues was competent enough. Consequently, Susan felt he was making it clear that he was the only one that she could work with. When Susan confronted the analyst with his unprofessional behaviour, he turned the interpretation around and put the onus on Susan to bear the burden of the boundary violation. His response was, "Oh, yes, I am aware that you are very sensitive." Susan was left to bear the psychological pain of the analyst's violation by his refusal to accept responsibility for his behaviour.

When Susan, now a therapist herself, retold her story, she was still filled with anger—even though the incident happened many years before our discussion. She felt as if she had been placed under a conspiracy of silence because of the unusual circumstances of the analysis, which she equated with a parent-child constellation. She wondered how she managed to get caught and how she was unable to notice what she now sees as absolutely obvious. In explanation, she said, "If you don't know anything different, then you think it's a normal situation."

This story raises a number of significant issues. The first is that the roles in the analysis were reversed, and Susan's interests and psychotherapeutic needs quickly took second priority to the immediate needs of the analyst. Further, Susan's ability to accurately judge the reality of the situation was greatly diminished. It was therefore very difficult for her to make a decision about what to do. Susan's last comment raises an important issue about the need to protect analysands who are uninformed about professional boundaries and ethical requirements relating to the psychotherapeutic frame. Rather than indulging their personal interests, members of the profession should act in ways that uphold the integrity of the profession, in the interests of all future and current clients.

2. The Story of Raina

The second case presents the story of Raina, a therapist of many years, who experienced non-sexual boundary violations with her male Jungian analyst. Raina was not a Jungian therapist, but she had read a book by Jung just before meeting the analyst and thought that a Jungian could give her some direction and meaning in her life that she was unable to experience through her own therapeutic orientation.

Raina stayed in analysis for several years and had a very positive transference to her analyst, as she experienced total and unconditional acceptance during sessions with him. It was an experience she had lacked in her childhood and now lacked in her marriage, and she found it very comforting. Her justifiable need to be in an environment where she could experience this unconditional acceptance also contributed to her inability to end the analysis sooner. She felt that the analyst really liked her, although there was no erotic or sexual energy between them. Raina now believes that the analyst identified with the archetype of the Healer, and as a result was psychologically inflated during most of the time that the analysis lasted. She reports that he would often say, "sometimes you have to break the rules for healing to occur," and that he openly disagreed with the need for codes of ethics. From the very beginning of the analysis, he initiated a series of boundary violations, which, in retrospect, Raina feels arose out of his personal loneliness and need for emotional intimacy. During sessions, he would often talk about his personal history, including his love life, and sometimes criticized other analysts in the community. He often invited Raina to social events or personally asked her to participate in groups that he was organizing. Sometimes Raina accepted and sometimes she declined. During the first year, he also asked to borrow money from her. Raina felt that she was unfairly put into the position of having to make a decision, a psychological situation characteristic of the double bind described above. She feared that if she said no, he would abandon her or his feelings would be hurt.

The boundary violations increased progressively. When her husband was experiencing significant psychological distress, she brought a dream which the analyst interpreted as meaning that her husband should also enter into analysis with him. Raina questioned this, but he said he had analyzed members of the same family before to good effect. However, when the analyst began independently analyzing her husband, it became clear to her that he now knew information about Raina's married life that he could only have known through work with her husband. She felt there was significant blurring between the two analyses.

The ending of the analysis and Raina's significant loss of faith in Jungian analysis came at a particularly vulnerable time in her life. She had just lost someone very close to her, and was in a state of grief. In addition, she had made significant changes to her personal living circumstances. It was thus a time in her life when, due to a series of devastating losses, she was particularly vulnerable and psychically fragile, and so greatly needed the support of her analyst.

Within two weeks of the tragic events affecting Raina, during the last ten minutes of one analytic session, the analyst confessed to her that he had fallen in love with another female analysand and wanted her opinion as to what he should do. Raina fell into her therapist role and became her analyst's analyst during a session that Raina was paying for. She had the impression that she was not the only one he had consulted and that he had also asked other members of his professional community. The analyst had been advised against entering into the relationship with the analysand, and Raina was strong in echoing this concern. Despite all this advice, however, the analyst entered into a sexual relationship with the client before his analytic sessions with her were over.

Because Raina was a participant in a group led by the analyst, she quickly discovered the identity of the other analysand and knew that her analyst had dismissed all the warnings he'd received. As a therapist herself, Raina knew the ethical prohibitions against entering into these kinds of relationships. As she put it: "My faith was broken and I left the analysis in deep emotional pain and feeling very betrayed." When I asked her to identify the worst part of the experience, she said, "The whole experience was very disillusioning for me, especially concerning my esteem for Jungians. I lost respect for someone whom I once respected a great deal. There was also the damage to several important relationships that I found through him. I think it was because this was such a major issue for me. Now I feel only contempt for him."

3. The Story of Nick

The final case is a composite reflecting the degree to which an analyst can exploit the analytic situation to meet her personal business needs. I will call the client Nick. When Nick began his therapy with his female analyst, he felt an immediate affinity with her. This was not Nick's first analytic experience, but his previous analysts had been men. He felt it was time to work with a woman.

The erosion of the analytic frame began during the very first hour and continued throughout the analysis. The analyst was consistently late for every session—usually twenty minutes to half an hour, but occasionally as much as forty-five minutes to an hour. Nick was deeply disturbed by this, although he knew it was happening with every analysand. After several weeks, Nick mentioned his concerns. The analyst dismissed them, ascribing Nick's insecurities and despair to "your negative mother complex." Despite the discussion and repeated expressions of concern, nothing changed. Likely to compensate for the lateness, Nick was given extra time, and several sessions ran close to two hours, though he only paid for one hour. In addition, sessions tended to open with a general discussion of politics or the current state of the economy, which took up nearly twenty minutes of the hour. Nick was in the financial industry and felt that the analyst initiated these discussions to get information and investment advice. Nick felt that these discussions were unrelated to his inner process and life.

The structural problems in the analytic setting put Nick in a double bind early on in the process. He experienced a great deal of anxiety when waiting. He was an extremely busy man and yet found that he accommodated the analyst's schedule. He felt that he eroded his own sense of power by being submissive and passive in the situation, while inside he was angry and resentful. Nevertheless, he felt special because of the extra time given at the end of the sessions and was afraid that if he complained too much about the lateness, he would have to settle for shorter sessions. Such a situation did not secure trust in the analytic container, and the problems with the frame contributed to a growing distrust of the analyst. Nick felt paralyzed and unable to leave.

Over the course of the analysis, the list of boundary violations grew. About a year into the sessions, the analyst began initiating calls outside sessions. These discussions mainly involved the analyst asking for financial or business advice. Whenever Nick would broach the subject of what was going on in the relationship, the analyst would retreat into a more formal analytic tone, apparently unable to talk about these dynamics. Nick said he was left very confused and often fell into a depression after these extra phone calls.

As the analysis developed, Nick was continually asked for business advice and expertise on a wide range of matters during and outside the sessions. More than once, the analyst asked Nick if he would be interested in becoming her business manager. In addition, she requested computer assistance and help with various visual presentations that she was making. At times, Nick felt that the analyst was placing more emphasis on these activities than on the therapeutic work, and he began to realize that, in fact, these requests were becoming part of the analytic process. When Nick confronted her about them, the analyst failed to respond in a way that made sense to Nick: once, the analyst replied, "it was convenient"; another time, the analyst questioned why these activities were unacceptable, leaving Nick speechless. During this part of the analysis, Nick felt that he carried the role of business partner, advisor, and confidante, in addition to his role as analysand.

Like the other two analysts, Nick's analyst openly criticized the other analysts in the community. Nick also discovered that the analyst made comments like this openly to her other analysands. To a large extent, the analyst had isolated herself professionally from the analytic community of which she was part. She often said that she felt more sense of community among her analysands than among her professional colleagues.

Nick felt a growing psychological tension and anger at being placed in this dual role. His previous analytic experience had told him that the analytic container needed to be protected. At the same time, he felt protective of the relationship. Because he was fond of the analyst and lacked close women friends other than his wife, he wanted to move the analytic relationship into a personal realm after the analysis was over. This was one of the reasons he felt he couldn't leave.

When the analyst complained to Nick about the boundary violations of other analysts, he didn't understand why there was a difference between what the other analysts did and what was happening in this analysis. He confronted the analyst about this, but the analyst repeatedly said that she didn't have a problem with the boundaries. She claimed that her requests of Nick were only superficial violations and that she always tried "to give everyone what they needed." Nick felt that there was a gap between what the analyst said and how she behaved. When Nick continued to question this, he was accused of being too demanding and even of being abusive. In her own defense, the analyst maintained that the requests for assistance were not made out of self-interest and that they were part of the therapeutic process. When Nick confronted the analyst about things she said, the analyst would change her story. For instance, she rationalized her requests for personal business assistance by saying things like " I wanted to see how competent you are" or, at worst, "It was just a joke. Can't it be a joke?" These responses only emphasized the analyst's attempts to skirt around the issue of a hidden agenda and to pacify Nick's growing anger. Nick felt as if a big fog was descending around him, as he never knew what to believe and what to disbelieve. One could image that the worst part of the whole experience was that Nick's view of reality was being compromised because the analyst was never straight with him.

Issues Raised by the Case Studies

The three stories have several similarities. At some level, the analysands knew the analysis was over the moment the analyst initiated a change that was beyond the parameters of the protected space. The stories also show the wounding that the clients felt, even though the analysts were generally unaware that they had committed violations. The analysts did not likely hurt their clients on purpose, but they did have blind spots that they were acting out. Moreover, in those moments of unconsciousness, the violations undermined the integrity of the clients and of the analysis itself, creating confusion for the analysands in terms of their values and identity, and regarding the purpose and direction of the analytic work.

The portrayal of the analysts reveal interesting similarities. Each analyst let his or her personal needs take precedence over the needs of the client and failed to honour the rigours of the profession. When confronted with their behaviour, they resorted to denial and rationalization to protect their self-image. These analysts were also isolated from their colleagues and in all cases actively criticized them to their analysands. Their inability to accept responsibility for their actions left their clients to carry the burden of the violation and the emotional pain that came with it.

When analysts deny that a violation has taken place or rationalize their transgressing behaviour, their motivation to do so is compounded by the need for self-protection and because of the terror of losing their livelihood and reputation. Denial is a powerful psychological mechanism that helps protect one's self-image and works to save the ego from the experience of shame, guilt, and embarrassment. Increasingly, clients who have been the victims of boundary violations need to seek redress through civil law suits and regulatory bodies because analysts have failed to accept responsibility for their behaviour. But this situation creates a vicious circle. Collective redress increases the negative consequences of being found guilty of boundary violations and reinforces the self-protective mechanisms of denial and rationalization.

Falling prey to the pull of the unconscious is a necessary part of the individuation process and of becoming conscious. It is through this that we become aware of our psychic landscape and of the dynamics of the particular complex that holds us in its grasp at any given time. Often, we need outside assistance to restore the ego to its position of objectivity—that is, some outside force must highlight the discrepancy between the facts of the world and our distorted perception of them when under the influence of a complex.

৯▲

In light of the moral ideal of individuation as an ethical process and the definition of integrity presented in Part I, it is vital to give precedence to moral considerations over self-interest. The moral values of consciousness, integrity, and compassion are needed to heal boundary violations in the professional–client relationship. On the other hand, actions of self-protection give priority to self-interest, rather than to integrity, the Heart, and individuation, and this adds to the wound caused by the original violation. Offending analysts who are confronted with their archetypal Shadow are humbled, and they feel shame and embarrassment because they realize the truth that their actions do not measure up to the ideals identified by the profession. However, healing can take place when both analytic partners become aware of re-enactments of unconscious material. For this to occur, the analyst and the analysand need to call upon the ego's strength and courage to carry out the ethical confrontation with the unconscious. Marilyn Peterson writes:

> The client gains clarity when professionals give information that makes order out of what happened. The client gains safety when professionals no longer avoid exploring the truth about themselves and assume responsibility for who they are. The client gains more control when professionals rebalance the relationship by acknowledging the wrong and holding themselves accountable. The client gains validation that releases him or her from the violation when professionals face their shame and accept the consequences of their behaviour.[21]

---

21   Peterson, *At Personal Risk*, p. 163.

Part III

෨

The Ethical Attitude

CHAPTER 8

Suffering and the Ethical Attitude

Because individuation is a heroic and often tragic task, the most difficult of
all, it involves suffering.[1]

—C.G. Jung

Introduction

Jung's psychological view of conscience as the "Voice of God" sent us on this
journey into individuation as an ethical process, and has been the catalyst for
an exploration of ethics in analysis. Conscience, for Jung, was distinct from
the "common stock of moral thou-shall nots" —the moral standards we inherit
from parental and other authority figures, which correspond to Freud's notion
of the "superego." Jung saw conscience as extending beyond such inherited
rules, residing instead in the psychological principle of the Divine Voice
within that guides our individuation process.

This view of conscience contains a challenge, however, as it is sometimes
difficult to determine what is the "Voice of God" and what is not. Dreams, for
instance, do not present themselves as emanating from any "one true voice." As
manifestations of the unconscious and compensations for a one-sided attitude
of the ego, dreams can stand in moral judgement or they can graphically present a litany of immoral behaviour. The content of our dreams depends on our
conscious attitude; the unconscious will stand in opposition to the ego's stance.

---

1   C.G. Jung, *Psychology and Religion: West and East*, Vol. 11 of *The Collected Works* (Princeton, NJ: Princeton University Press, 1969), paragraph 233.

Jung's conflict of duty—or, in modern language, his ethical dilemma—makes it clear that the subject matter offered by the unconscious is not straightforward or simple, and that when we work with the unconscious, either as clients or as analysts, we face significant moral challenges. This challenge lies in determining the motivation for our thoughts, actions, and behaviour. Jung highlights this when he writes:

> If we obey the judgement of conscience, we stand-alone and have hearkened to a subjective voice, not knowing what the motives are on which it rests. No one can guarantee that he has only noble motives.[2]

> The view of conscience as the Voice of God becomes an extremely delicate problem. In practice, it is very difficult to indicate the exact point at which the "right" conscience stops and the "false" one begins, and what the criterion is that divides one from the other.[3]

In Jung's reflections, we also find the resolution to his "conflict of duty" that originated with the vision of the turd falling on Basel Cathedral—that is, a conception of the God-image that contained the polarities of light and dark, good and evil.

"If the *vox Dei* conception is correct," writes Jung,

> we are faced logically with a metaphysical dilemma: either there is a dualism, and God's omnipotence is halved, or the opposites are contained in the monotheistic God-image, as for instance in the Old Testament image of Yahweh, which shows us morally contradictory opposites existing side by side.[4]

Jung's vision of individuation contains such an ethical, or metaphysical, dilemma, and in the remaining pages, we will focus on the ethical attitude[5] needed to deal with this dilemma. The essential questions are: How can we approach living individuation as an ethical process? What is the attitude that

---

2   C.G. Jung, "A Psychological View of Conscience" in *Civilization in Transition.*, Vol. 10 of *The Collected Works* (Princeton, NJ: Princeton University Press, 1969), paragraph 837.

3   *Ibid.*, paragraph 840.

4   *Ibid.*, paragraph 844.

5   The concept of the "ethical attitude" referred to here has been used in this context by English analyst Hester McFarland Solomon.

we must have? What signs do we follow? What messages do we heed? How do we integrate individuation as an ethical process with ethics in analysis?

The ethical dimension of Jung's vision of individuation is that we must assume conscious responsibility for our psychological growth toward wholeness, think with our hearts and feel with our heads, and learn to live with the ambiguity of the in-between space between collective moral precepts and our own subjective experience of our actions. Although this moral challenge demands a commitment to discovering and living one's unique pattern of wholeness or destiny, Jung did not see the individuation journey as an endeavour achieved alone, in isolation from the rest of the world. Psychological growth is achieved in relationship to the outer world, as well as to the inner world. The journey, therefore, necessarily involves an encounter with the Other, and the nature of the ethical discourse involves consciously entering a dialogue with this Other. The exchange serves to bring the opposites between self and the Other into view, and presents the moral challenge of coming to terms with the Shadow. As Hester McFarland Solomon, a senior training analyst in London, puts it, "in order to fulfil its ethical function, the self must recognize the substantive reality and subjectivity of the other."[6]

The hypothesis is that the attitude required to live the ethical challenges of the individuation process is the same for the analysand who embarks on the individuation journey and for the analyst who accompanies that person on their journey. By virtue of their own encounters with the unconscious through their own analyses, analysts impart this ethical attitude to their analysands and training candidates more by their being than by what they say.

Our Attitude toward Suffering

The etymology of the word *suffer* originates from the Latin meaning "to bear" or "to carry". From Helen Luke[7], we get an image of *an undercarriage which bears the weight of a vehicle above the wheels*, alluding to the psychological experience of carrying the weight of our sins or transgressions. The decisive factor in our ethical attitude toward life is our attitude toward suffering and whether we suffer in a neurotic/meaningless way or in a meaningful, conscious way. In the former, we carry the weight unconsciously. Thus our suffering appears as symptoms of depression, anxiety or self-pity. The repression of unacceptable

---

6   Hester McFarland Solomon, "The Ethical Attitude in Analytic Training and Practice" (paper presented to the Ethics Matters Conference, Cambridge, July 2003), p. 4.

7   Helen Luke, *Old Age* (Colorado Springs, CO: Image Books, 1996).

or distasteful ideas and thoughts is the source of neurosis and meaningless suffering. Jung writes:

> Repression has the apparent advantage of clearing the conscious mind of worry, and the spirit of all its troubles, but to counter that, it causes an indirect suffering from something unreal, namely a neurosis. Neurotic suffering is an unconscious fraud and has no moral merit as has real suffering.[8]

For example, one effect of collective—that is, societal—repression has been to place the onus of moral responsibility on abuse victims, while the aggressors in positions of power and affluence are granted immunity. In this moral system, suffering becomes polarized and full of dualities. Sickness, vulnerability, and failure are regarded as sins and as punishment for the inability to live up to certain heroic ideals. Consequently, anything deemed unacceptable to this system is relegated to the unconscious and the Shadow. In a dominant cultural ethos, which over-identifies with collective values of the hero, we then have a "good conscience" when we are in harmony with values deemed to be positive and acceptable by the collective. Conversely, we have a "bad conscience" when we are not in harmony with them.

Psychologically, however, the identification with the "hero" creates two psychic systems, whereby the persona is aligned with societal values and the Shadow (containing all that is deemed unacceptable) is split off. Suffering becomes neurotic through the suppression or repression of undesirable material, and the undesirable material becomes projected onto some Other. The neurotic sufferer is unable to accept that material as his or her own and is filled with bitter resentments, black moods and depression.

The projected Shadow is then discharged via an external "scapegoat," who carries the unwanted elements of the personality and the unconscious conflict. The image of the Scapegoat comes from the Jewish story connected with the Yom Kippur ritual of atonement and the riddance of evil. The ritual, described in Leviticus 16:20–22, involves the sacrifice of the scapegoat and its exile into the desert: "The goat shall carry all iniquities of the Israelites upon itself into some barren wasteland and the man shall let it go there in the wilderness." This ritual serves to extract and exile the sin and guilt of the group, which accompany the group's sense of having transgressed some moral code. The goat therefore holds and carries this knowledge, and is banished into the uncon-

---

8　C.G. Jung, *The Development of Personality*, Vol. 17 of *The Collected Works*. (Princeton, NJ: Princeton University Press, 1954), paragraph 154.

scious. The symbol illustrates a condition whereby an individual falls out of a state of oneness with the collective and its shared values. Through the banishment ritual, it becomes possible for the members of the community to stand purified and united with each other in their identification with group values. The attitude toward abuse long held by Western society might be understood through this scapegoat dynamic: the group unconsciously identifies individuals who bear the burden of its sins and then casts them out into the desert.

Over the last several decades, Western society has slowly released the veil of repression from various kinds of power abuses—including those by therapists and analysts—and has increased its awareness of their devastating psychological effects. As a result, significant changes have occurred in public attitudes and social policy. While it has been necessary to magnify the plight of victims in order to change cultural perceptions of abusive situations, the opposite situation has now been constellated in a pendulum effect that has caused the "archetype of the Victim" to predominate. In this constellation, the duality of "victim" and "perpetrator" is clear. However, the victim is usually portrayed as innocent and as having a somewhat diminished capacity to determine the outcome of the experience, thus being robbed of the efficacy to deal with it. Conversely, the perpetrator is portrayed as the instrument of evil. In this moral system, the victim is not seen as having a role in the injury that has befallen him or her, and is thereby absolved of the legal responsibility associated with the incident. Thus the victim is held free of moral guilt in terms of the cause of his or her suffering, and the pursuit of justice and monetary compensation or some kind of other concrete result is considered a sufficient redress. Such an attitude projects onto the Other the total responsibility for the situation and looks to that Other for some reparation as the source of redemption from the suffering. As author Tanya Wilkinson suggests in her book *Persephone Returns*, "the disquieting ugly aspects of victimization are perceived as manifesting solely in the 'other,' who must change them."[9]

It seems that a reconciliation is needed between the perspective that the victim bears all responsibility and the perspective that the perpetrator bears all responsibility. This need echoes a desire for healing and for truth, a need to transcend the duality of "us" and "them," of "victim" and "perpetrator" It might be possible to find a clue about to proceed in the spiritual origins of the words *victim* and *sacrifice*.

9   Tanya Wilkinson, *Persephone Returns* (Berkeley, CA: Pagemill Press, 1996), p. 10.

Victim

Originally, the word *victim* was used to describe the situation in religious sacrifices where something or someone was offered up to a deity. Many ancient civilizations practised this kind of ritual in attempts to please, appease or show gratitude toward the gods. One of the most gruesome of these rituals was practised by the ancient Aztecs, who sacrificed human victims by cutting into their hearts, believing that the gods desired the spirit located in the blood. If the gods were not appeased and honoured, they thought, the sun would stop moving. In many cases, the victims in these rituals were prisoners of war or slaves; subject to the power of their captors/owners, they were sacrificed against their will. In other cases, victims of these sacrifices volunteered, considering themselves honoured to be chosen. The acts of brutality associated with these rituals took on a moral dignity, as they were considered to be done in the service of a noble or divine cause. The perpetrator of these sacrificial acts thus remained blameless and retained a position of moral integrity.

Whether in the service of a perceived divine act or because of some senseless brutality, the "victim" includes elements of sacrifice and powerlessness—that is, the circumstances are not brought about by the individual's free will or choice. Roger Fjellström, a philosopher at the University of Umeå in Sweden, suggests that the experience of victimhood is a relative and complex state of being which affects several capabilities of acting and living in the world. He offers us a way to understand this state by highlight the distinction between an "autonomy victim" and an "integrity victim."[10] In the case of an *autonomy victim*, the individual loses the ability to exercise her will because of external circumstances that prevent her from influencing the situation. In such a case, the self-determining autonomy of the individual has been cancelled out. In the situation of an *integrity victim*, the individual no longer has the capacity to make decisions for himself and is therefore unable to function normally. This individual usually functions in a reduced and often self-destructive way—likely because of some internal factor. The individual's integrity or wholeness (that is, the individual's sense of Self) is in some way compromised or distorted.

If we look at this state of victimhood in light of the power of the unconscious, we realize that we can indeed become "victims" of it in the way Fjellström suggests. It does not matter whether we are taken over by a complex

---

10   Roger Fjellström, *On Victimhood*, http://www.umu.se/philos/personal/fjellstrom/fjellstrom_eng.htm, 2002.

or caught in some archetypal identification, or whether we actively surrender to the process of fulfilling our destiny; our ability to exercise our ego will in the world is diminished. In other words, the ego—that is, the centre of consciousness and the part of the personality that is in the world—is unable to be self-determining, and ultimately cannot be the total master of its house.

These are the threads that surround the notions of victim, sacrifice, and surrender, and they are important elements in the ethical component of the individuation process. Are we victims of the individuation process or are we consciously surrendering to a higher spiritual purpose, much in the same way that "victims" of ancient sacrificial rites surrendered to gods? Jung's recognition that, at some level, the ego must give way to something bigger, can be encapsulated in the phrase, "the experience of the Self is always a defeat of the ego."[11]

For the purposes of this argument, the problem lies in the definition of "victim psychology," which can result in a person abdicating responsibility for her suffering. If followed to its extreme, the victim does not acknowledge her ability to transform herself (i.e., heal herself) from abusive and traumatic experiences, and to make sense of particular circumstances. This healing capacity is therefore unavailable to her. Suffering becomes neurotic and meaningless and the "victim" re-enacts the powerlessness of the original situation in another form. The duality of good and evil, and of the ego and the Shadow, is then reinforced.

Meaningful Suffering and the Transcendent Function

Emotional pain arising from hurt, loss, and death is part of the human journey. No one can escape the suffering that results from conflicts, failures, and the limitations of being human and living in the world. This kind of suffering is a fundamental element of the human condition. If approached with an attitude of engagement for the purpose of conscious awareness, suffering can be a major catalyst for psychological change and individuation. For Jung, this engagement lay at the very heart of the individuation journey:

> And because individuation is an heroic and often tragic task, the most difficult of all, it involves suffering, a passion of the ego: the ordinary, empirical man we once were is burdened with the fate of losing himself in

---

11   C.G. Jung, *Mysterium Coniunctionis*, Vol. 14 of *The Collected Works* (Princeton, NJ: Princeton University Press, 1970), paragraph 778.

a greater dimension and being robbed of his fancied freedom of will. He suffers, so to speak, from the violence done to him by the Self.[12]

It is our attitude toward suffering that determines whether it is meaningless or can have a redemptive quality. Meaningless or neurotic suffering results in the projection of unwanted material onto the world, and the neurotic sufferer may experience some fateful event which confronts them with the need for individuation from the outside. He or she may also experience the suffering in a symbolic form, through depression, anxiety, self-pity, shame, guilty, or a psychosomatic illness. Without a conscious understanding of this type of suffering, many people turn to various forms of medication in an attempt to alleviate the symptoms.

Helen Luke suggests that "there is no cure for inferior so-called suffering except a greater kind of suffering."[13] Our suffering can be redemptive, if we take the attitude that there is some meaning to it—that is, that it serves a purpose in individuation, psychological development, and the realization of wholeness, and rests in the "basic assumption that all things come from God, i.e. reflect a transpersonal purpose and meaning."[14] If we take an ethical attitude toward conscious suffering, we acknowledge that when our suffering originates from an "authentic" cause, we are led to experiences of spiritual enrichment and meaning. When we "integrate" consciousness with unconscious material, we can come to understand our place in the world and experience the divine and the numinous.

Helen Luke suggests that "real suffering belongs to innocence, not guilt."[15] It is only here that authentic transformation can occur. This requires full acceptance of suffering without false guilt, remorse or self-pity. This is also the point Jungian analyst Polly Young-Eisendrath makes when she writes: "Honest confrontation with this deeper anguish over our ordinary human limitations and imperfections, our inevitable loss, illness, decline and death, wakes us to the significance of our lives."[16] And according to author and psychoanalyst Irvin Yalom:

---

12   C.G. Jung, *Psychology and Religion: West and East*, paragraph 233.
13   Helen Luke, *Old Age*, p. 104.
14   Edward Edinger, *Ego and Archetype* (Boston, MA: Shambhala, 1992), p. 78.
15   Helen Luke, *Old Age*, p. 104.
16   Polly Young-Eisendrath, *The Resilient Spirit: Transforming Suffering into Insight and Renewal* (Reading, MA: Addison-Wesley Publishing, 1996), p. 9.

... engagement in life, a wilful and autonomously chosen "leap into commitment and action" is the only real cure available for one's own suffering, the only way in which authentic meaning can be generated in the face of the powerlessness of suffering. The meaning of human suffering is found, then, in the wilful act of the autonomous subject resolutely choosing to forge meaning and value in the midst of anguish and powerless passivity.[17]

The image of Christ's crucifixion gives us a poignant symbol of the suffering emerging from the ethical dimensions of individuation. The cross is one of four basic symbols in the human lexicon. The other three are the centre, the circle, and the square—and the composition of the cross, with its two arms at right angles meeting in a centre, creates a link to the other three. With the ends of the two arms corresponding to the four directions, the cross is a symbol of totality and wholeness that unites the opposites of heaven and earth, the divine and the human. Our language embodies this when we say we have "a cross to bear" or feel "nailed to the cross," suggesting that the image continues to have a powerful psychological presence. Taking up one's own cross involves consciously accepting and carrying the commitment to realize one's own particular pattern of wholeness,[18] as Christ's crucifixion reflects the fulfilment of his particular destiny. Christ carrying his cross to his "sacrificial" death and subsequent resurrection can be viewed psychologically as reflecting the "sacrificial" death of an old life, attitude, or perspective, which leads to a rebirth and the emergence of the new.

Jung saw Christ's crucifixion as a reflection of the moral suffering required in the individuation process when the ego and the Self are suspended in the tension of the opposites. The ego, as the centre of individual consciousness and identity, is suspended in the paradox of human duality; the Self, as the divine centre within, brings its eternal divinity and un-manifest existence into human and temporal reality. But both suffer—because the ego needs the Self in order to live meaningfully, while the Self needs the ego to live its experiment in life.[19] As Edward Edinger describes it:

At times, the transpersonal totality must be fed by the sacrificial blood of the ego. At other times, the ego cannot survive unless it finds contact with

---

17   Quoted in Edwin Gantt, "Levinas, Psychotherapy and the Ethics of Suffering," *Journal of Humanistic Psychology* 40 (Summer, 2000), p. 10.

18   Edinger, *Ego and Archetype*, p. 135.

19   Nathan Schwartz-Salant, *Narcissism and Character Transformation* (Toronto: Inner City Books, 1982), p. 120.

the life-promoting effects of the sacrificial blood of the Self.... Christ is both God and man i.e. both Self and ego. In terms of the sacrificial rite, he is both sacrificial priest and the sacrificial victim.[20]

Sacrifice

Integral to the individuation journey is the element of "sacrifice." The word *sacrifice* has its roots in the notion of *making sacred*, and, as described above, it is connected with offering something to the gods. When faced with a trauma, our ethical attitude will determine whether we succumb to a victim psychology or dedicate ourselves to meaningful sacrifice, surrendering ourselves to our destiny. It is the ethical attitude that binds the notions of victim, sacrifice, and surrender. The ethical attitude involved in meaningful suffering calls us to be actively engaged with life and to acknowledge that life transitions require change and new approaches. This demand for change also requires conscious sacrifice. Some aspect of the personality must be sacrificed to the gods: a cherished attitude; an expectation; a belief; a way of being in the world; a perception; or the old Self that is no longer life-serving. As with any loss, we must also consciously grieve that which has been sacrificed.

It is in the conscious experience of suffering that we have the opportunity to experience the transcendent function, grace, and the true *vox Dei*, the "Voice of God." From this perspective, we can now understand Jung's assertion that the solution to conflicts of conscience and moral conflicts of duty cannot come from the collective but must come from somewhere within the individual.

In his original 1916 article "The Transcendent Function,"[21] Jung imagined a function that bridged consciousness and the unconscious. This *transcendent function* arises spontaneously and organically from the unconscious because of the collision of the opposites as a dynamic "third," or synthesizing element, that facilitates the transition from one attitude to a new perspective. It provides the reconciling symbol for any pair of opposites and does so without negating either side of the conflict, doing justice instead to both. Jung describes the emergence of the numinous quality as "possessing authority not unjustly characterized as the Voice of God."[22] "The nature of the solution is in accord with

---

20   Edinger, *Ego and Archetype*, p. 241.
21   C.G. Jung, "The Transcendent Function" in *The Structure and Dynamics of the Psyche*, Vol. 8 of *The Collected Works* (Princeton, NJ: Princeton University Press, 1969), paragraphs 131–193.
22   C.G. Jung, "A Psychological View of Conscience," paragraph 856.

the deepest foundations of the personality as well as its wholeness; it embraces conscious and unconscious, and therefore transcends the ego."[23]

This synthesizing element is important because it possesses the power to fashion a solution that was previously unknown or unavailable to consciousness. Through a symbol, we gain new insight or develop a new attitude to the conflict that we could not have imagined before. This allows for psychological development and evolution. As Jung writes in *Mysterium Coniunctionis*:

> For you only feel yourself on the right road when the conflicts of duty seem to have resolved themselves, and you have become the victim of a decision made over your head or in defiance of your heart.[24]

> From this we can see the numinous power of the self that can hardly be experienced in any other way. For this reason, the experience of the self is always a defeat for the ego.[25]

The experience of the transcendent function and of the numinous power of the Self is an experience of *grace*. Taken in the religious context, *grace* suggests being protected and sanctified by the favour or gift of God. Jung often wrote that analytic work succeeds by the grace of God, but that the individual must yield to the Self's wisdom. With the phrase *Deo concedente*, Jung recognized that the real nature of the psychic process was a mystery that transcended consciousness:

> If the work succeeds, it often works like a miracle, and one can understand what it was that prompted the alchemists to insert a heartfelt *Deo concedente* in their recipes or to allow that only if God wrought a miracle could their procedure be brought to a successful conclusion.[26]

Through the transcendent function and grace, we have the psychological experience of psychic peace and contentment, and of being moved by something larger than we are. Psychic energy is released from the conflict as unconscious issues reach the point where they can be integrated and projections made

---

23   *Ibid.*
24   In this case, Jung is using the term *heart* in connection with passions or desires.
25   C.G. Jung, *Mysterium Coniunctionis*, paragraph 778.
26   C.G. Jung, *The Practice of Psychotherapy*, Vol. 16 of *The Collected Works* (Princeton, NJ: Princeton Univeristy Press, 1966), paragraph 385.

conscious. The resolution of the conflict comes from the appearance of the *reconciling motif*. Often this motif is that of the returning orphan or abandoned child in a dream—the innocent part of us that now has the opportunity to be seen, to authentically suffer and to be received with compassion. It is this child who has returned from the journey and who carries both the split-off part of the personality and a new image of the Self. In describing this resolution of the tension of the opposites, the authors of *A Critical Dictionary of Jungian Analysis* write: "rather than opposition, there now appears a new born configuration, symbolic of the nascent whole, a figure possessing potential beyond those that the conscious mind has yet been able to conceive."[27] This experience of grace cannot be reached or created by an act of will but it occurs when the redeeming qualities of suffering and sacrifice unite.

The Ethical Attitude for Individuation

What ethical attitude is needed in our personal journeys as we cope with the limitations of our lives, injuries, betrayals, and injustices? How do we approach our individuation processes? In his own work with clients, Jung did not focus on fashioning a cure that would leave the client free of any subsequent difficulties. Rather, he viewed analysis as emphasizing adjustments in attitude: with the help of the analyst, clients could learn how to cope with and navigate through life's difficulties. He also saw life as a journey that requires us to undergo periodic renewal as we pass through the various stages of youth, middle age, and old age. Each stage requires adaptation to changing life circumstances. In addition, Jung addressed the central question "What kind of mental and moral attitude is it necessary to have towards the disturbing influences of the unconscious, and how can it be conveyed to the patient?"[28]

This attitude is the one that we develop with respect to our own unique individuation journey. It reflects the degree to which we take responsibility for our lives, accept the truth of who we are, and live genuinely in the world. The ethical attitude calls us to live in "right relationship" to our inner and outer lives. The "victim psychology" described above does not assume this responsibility but instead projects the power to heal or redeem the suffering soul onto some Other. As such, the "victim" remains essentially powerless in life and without efficacy. Living the ethical dimension of individuation requires

---

27   Andrew Samuels, Bani Shorter, and Fred Plaut, *A Critical Dictionary of Jungian Analysis* (London: Routledge, 1986), p. 103.

28   Jung, *The Structure and Dynamics of the Psyche*, paragraph 144.

that we adopt an active engagement with life's struggles and recognize how powerful our attitudes and beliefs are in our experience. This is one of individuation's major moral challenges. We must recognize that we are co-creators of our problems through the autonomous will of our complexes and the natural tendency of the unconscious to project itself onto the world.

Polly Young-Eisendrath brings this perspective to the understanding of the ethical attitude when she writes: "This is the difference between hell and heaven as we recognize that our own responses, our attitudes, are the powerful lenses of reality in the way in which we affect others and evoke responses from them"[29]. She believes that, "knowing our responsibility for our thoughts and feelings while holding the tension of a conflict or a conflicted moment within ourselves, we can move beyond our habits, our complexes, and our immediate suffering into discovery and development."[30]

The ability to reflect ethically on our lives implies, according to Young-Eisendrath, the ability to "think abstractly about our experiences, tracing causal lines from our thoughts, feelings and intentions, to our actions, and from our actions to their consequences."[31] It also requires that an individual has worked on themselves enough so that the ego possesses sufficient strength, has assumed its position as the centre of consciousness, and is the carrier of the person's identity. This seems to be a necessary condition in order to experience our "I"-ness—a feeling of being centred—and our integrity (wholeness) and authenticity. This ability and conscious reflection frees us from the childish impulses of unconscious complexes that often drive our behaviour and actions. However, the process means that the ego must admit that, at times, it is maladjusted, infantile, limited, and imperfect.

Do we acquire an ethical attitude as a result of our childhood development and then retain it, intact, throughout the rest of our lives? Or do we need to consciously develop our ethical attitude throughout our lives? As previously discussed in the chapter on moral development, our ethical attitude derives partially from our innate moral disposition and partially from our experience of early caregivers, social values, and education. The theories of moral development advanced by Piaget, Kohlberg, Gilligan, and Erikson suggest that the acquisition of an ethical attitude is part of a later stage of development related to the tasks of adolescence and early adulthood. Specifically, Erik Erikson defines ethical responsibility as a mature ethical orientation encompassing a

---

29   Young-Eisendrath, *The Resilient Spirit*, p. 147.
30   *Ibid.*, p. 156.
31   *Ibid.*, p. 141.

combination of responsibility, values, and beliefs, and a philosophy of life that is fully developed only in adulthood.

As individuation is an ongoing process, and as we are constantly met with new challenges, we can expect to experience new confrontations with the unconscious and never-ending conflicts of duty. Is our ethical capacity constant? Steven Greisdorf, a leader in thinking about ethics in businesses, suggests that building ethical capacity involves an ongoing process of strengthening one's ability to make ethical decisions: "Ethical capacity is constantly being developed taking into account new information, new learning, new experience, new relationships and new understanding. As such, our ethical capacity, like our muscles, must be exercised."[32] This statement suggests that ethical capacity is not something we acquire through any kind of developmental achievement, to be retained for the rest of our lives. Ethical reflections are not static endeavours; they are dynamic and ever-present.

Greisdorf advocates four key elements in the process of ethical capacity building: *listening, reflecting, discussing,* and *engaging.* These elements embody the need for both an internal and an external orientation—a perspective that was also advocated in Neumann's *New Ethic* (see Chapter 5). The elements also reflect the need to be actively engaged in discussion with the Other, whoever or whatever that Other happens to be. The ethical attitude does not operate in isolation. To function properly, it must rely on the concept of "right relationship." That is, we can only come to know our ethical capacity in relationship to another.

Similarly, Greisdorf says that *listening* is an inner and an outer process. Listening means being open to our inner voice and conscience, while also heeding and noting the information we receive from outside. The second component of ethical capacity building is *reflecting*: we must constantly evaluate our ideas, beliefs, and ideals as they are either affirmed or challenged. This also compels us to reassess our beliefs and ideals in light of changing circumstances. Through the third component, *discussing*, we articulate our beliefs to the world as a process of delving more deeply into the subject. This allows us to clarify the impact or potential impact of our beliefs on our environment and the people in it. Finally, Greisdorf advocates the need to put the fruits of the first three processes to work—that is, we must bring them into the world, actively *engaging* in ethical capacity building on a daily basis. He suggests that engagement requires a degree of risk and a tolerance for ambiguity, uncertainty, and anxiety.

---

32   Steven D. Greisdorf, *Building Our Ethical Capacity* (Caux Initiatives for Business, 2000), http://www.cauxinitiativesforbusiness.org.

The Ethical Attitude in Analytic Practice

Until now, we have explored the attitude we need in order to live an ethical life and experience individuation as an ethical process. When translated to the analytic or therapeutic setting, the ethical attitude means holding the "right relationship" to that situation, in addition to recognizing the reality and subjectivity of the Other. The ethical attitude in analytic practice necessitates the understanding of the "analyst's responsibility to another regardless of whether the other sees their duties toward the analyst in the same way."[33]

While collective ethical codes provide a framework, it is impossible for these codes to account for every eventuality. Further, it is quite possible to adhere strictly to a collective ethical code and still behave unethically. As a result, the general public may become uncertain that analysts and therapists will behave ethically in the privacy of their offices, and may lose trust. That is why, as awareness of ethical violations in the helping professions grows, discussion of this issue will become increasingly important.

The ethical dilemmas that analysts face in day-to-day practice arise from the unique chemistry between the analyst and the client. This is where the ethical attitude must come into play. Because of the notable absence of studies of the ethical attitude in the analytic literature, Hester McFarland Solomon has written extensively about the issue. In several of her works, she challenges the assumption that as long as analysts follow stated ethical guidelines, they can consider themselves ethical. For her, the analytic attitude is an ethical attitude.

After years of reflection, Jung himself recognized the danger of following the "Voice of God" because it could come from either side of conscience. Therefore, he saw that a "special act of reflection" is required—especially in situations where the numinous or archetypal level of the psyche has been touched. He writes:

> As soon as the dialogue between two people touches on something fundamental, essential and numinous, and a certain rapport is felt, it gives rise to a phenomenon which Lévy-Bruhl fittingly called *participation mystique*. It is an unconscious identity in which two individual psychic spheres interpenetrate to such a degree that it is impossible to say what belongs to whom .... For this a special act of reflection is required.[34]

---

33   Solomon, *The Ethical Attitude in Analytic Training and Practice*, p. 4.
34   Jung, "A Psychological View of Conscience," paragraph 852.

The key phrase is Jung's reference to a "special act of reflection." His own attitude in his practice was that patience and fortitude are needed in order to wait for the appropriate or "solution destined" that will emerge from the tension of the opposites through this "reflection." Jung disdained convenient and unexamined assumptions that allowed the ego to remain inert in the one-sided conviction its rightness and correctness by projecting the unacceptable onto some Other. But Jung was also aware of the importance for analyst and analysand to avoid losing ego boundaries to the extent that they could be taken over by an apparent "Voice of God" and to fall into a *participation mystique*. The resulting ethic that demands a perspective on self and other that is difficult and painful to maintain.[35]

The analytic attitude is strikingly similar to the ethical attitude that analysts need to adopt in their confrontations with their own unconscious and in their own individuation processes. This position can be described as having "one foot in and one foot out of the analytic situation," remaining detached in the face of the powerful forces that can be constellated in the analytic work, while being present to and participating in the analytical relationship, thus ensuring that the working alliance is maintained. Remaining solely on the side of detachment results in empathic failure, while full immersion in the relationship results in a *participation mystique* and an unconscious collusion. The ethical analytic attitude involves maintaining a precarious balance between these opposite poles. The analyst needs to be centred and balanced, that is, he must remain in the heart of the Self, where the ego does not identify with either side of the opposites. As he must also be conscious of himself and of the Other, he must live in the space between consciousness and unconsciousness, in other words, in *Tao*.

The analytic attitude reflects an ongoing and conscientious effort to understand the conscious and unconscious factors present in the analytic relationship and to promote the psychological development of the client. It involves respect for the Other as he or she is, and maintaining the "right relationship" in the analytic dyad. By remaining in the tension of the opposites, the analyst refrains from reacting to the client's pressures or acting out. Instead the analyst must hold the space to allow for the natural unfoldment of the analysand's process.

In her article "Birth of the Ethical Attitude in a Clinical Setting," Elizabeth Richardson provides a useful analogy to describe the experience of falling out of the analytic attitude when a fundamental/archetypal level of the psyche

---

35   Beverley Zabriske, "Ethics," in *Jungian Analysis*, 2nd ed. (Chicago, IL: Open Court Publishing, 1995), p. 407.

is touched[36]. Her analogy is drawn from Homer's *Odyssey*: as Odysseus' ship passed the Island of the Sirens, he had himself strapped to its mast because the Sirens were known to lure sailors with a sweet but deceptive song, leading them to wreck their ships on the island's jagged rocks. The story offers an image of seduction and of being led away from straight and familiar paths. Richardson writes:

> It is at these times that we are most vulnerable and have to hope that our "internal sailors", our unconscious voices of reason will be lashing us to our own ethical mast and preventing us from being seduced into acting out with a patient. Hopefully, we will hear a warning note within informing us that something is at work in our unconscious that we need to be particularly mindful of.[37]

In Richardson's experience, anything that subverts the client's ability to look at his inner self and reflect on his own suffering is the work of the Sirens luring the analytic boat dangerously close to the rocks of destruction. In one version of the Siren's call, the analyst may fall for the analysand's attempts to avoid necessary suffering. The dangerous lure of being pushed into the unconscious by the analysand can mean unconsciously acting out. Analysts can easily fall into this in their efforts to be helpful.

How do analysts acquire their "ethical masts" and develop their ethical capacity? Analysts' ethical attitudes toward analysis are affected not only by influences experienced during childhood and early adulthood, but also by a number of factors occurring later in their lives. The analytical attitude begins to develop during the analyst's own personal analysis and grows further as a result of later experiences with training analysts. Through direct experience with the attitudes and behaviour of analysts and supervisors, candidates internalize distinct analytic attitudes. Examination of the genealogy of analytic training, for instance, has revealed that analysts are more likely to commit boundary violations with clients if their own analysts were found guilty of boundary violations.[38]

---

36 Elizabeth Richardson, "Birth of the Ethical Attitude in a Clinical Setting," in *The Ethical Attitude in Analytic Practice* (London: Free Association Press, 2003), pp. 65–79.

37 *Ibid.*, p. 65.

38 See Glen Gabbard and Eva Lester, *Boundaries and Boundary Violations in Psychoanalysis* (New York: Basic Books, 1995).

A candidate's ethical attitude will also be directly affected by the *ethos* of their training institute (i.e., the organization's culture and spirit, and the attitudes of its members),[39] and this collective ethos is the aggregate of the ethical attitudes of current and past members. If these values are not openly discussed, members and candidates could acquire an illusion of common governing principles where none actually exist. What is crucial here is that the ethical environment in which candidates are trained informs candidates' internalized professional attitudes toward the profession and toward the ethical treatment of their clients. The implications of this for training institutes are quite important.

How do analysts know when they have strayed too close to the rocks and the Sirens' island? What warning call will initiate the special act of reflection? Acting out is not always revealed through the analyst's or the client's dreams or in other kinds of messages from the unconscious. Adolf Guggenbühl-Craig suggests that truth is needed when dealing with the Shadow.[40] He argues that analysts, likewise, must be truthful when they are confronted with the professional Shadow.

> If a patient gets wind of this shadow, it is crucial for the further progress of the therapy that we be capable of admitting to him our own backsliding into the unconscious and the professional shadow, no matter how painful such an admission may be. The patient, after all, must also face up to painful insights. By constantly trying to spot the workings of our psychotherapeutic shadow, to catch it red-handed, we help our patients in their own confrontations with the dark brother. If we fail to do this, all the patient learns from us is how to fool himself and the world, and the value of analysis becomes highly questionable.[41]

Much in the same way that the transcendent function provides for the synthesis that springs from the analysand's suspension on the cross and the resolution of the tension of the opposites, analysts, according to Hester McFarland Solomon, need an *analytic third*—that is, an outside factor—to integrate material arising from the analytic work. In a paper presented to the first Ethics Matters Conference for the International Association for Ana-

---

39   Fiona Palmer Barnes, "Ethics in Practice" in *The Ethical Attitude of Analytic Practice* (London: Free Association Books, 2003), p. 42.

40   Adolf Guggenbühl-Craig, *Power in the Healing Professions* (Woodstock, CT: Spring Publications, 1971), p. 29.

41   *Ibid.*, p. 30.

lytical Psychologists,[42] Solomon argues that analysts must have an "internal protected space in which to process the psychic events" of the analysis, thus allowing time for Jung's "special act of reflection." Her argument is that supervision provides an analytic third. This contention is consistent with the results of the survey described in Chapter 8. The conclusion of this survey of analysts' attitudes was that analysts are free to follow their own consciences when faced with ethical dilemmas in their practices because of the peer support around them. The implication is that when contained within a community of peers, they feel comfortable bringing issues to colleagues before they feel compelled to act out. Peer supervision can be especially helpful in the difficult area of unconscious countertransference reactions that might lead to acting out and boundary violations. Supervision can take place with senior analysts, in peer supervision groups, or through other professional development activities, and it can serve to restore the ego's attitude if it has been lost to the control of a powerful complex. Hester McFarland Solomon writes:

> I wish to put forward the view that the provision of ongoing supervision throughout training and post qualification, provides a third area of analytic discourse, helping to ensure that both patient and analyst emerge out of the *Massa confusa* of the immediacy of the analytic relationship, an important instance of "progressive triangulation" creating the "third space" necessary for mental growth and development.[43]

Solomon claims that supervision or "triangulated space" is necessary for the maintenance of the analytic attitude. The "triangulated space" offers room for the "special act of reflection" and opportunity to think about a third—the Other—whether that Other is the client, an idea, a concept, or any manifestation of the unconscious. Solomon suggests that this idea has profound implications for training institutes, which need to foster the internalization of a "third space" in training candidates rather than assessing candidates only according to their ability to work independently:

> Fostering the ethical expectation of ongoing supervisory provision is more likely to engender a generationally based commitment to the analytic attitude within a training institution, as the tradition of good clinical practice is passed down across the analytic training generations.[44]

---

42   Solomon, "The Ethical Attitude in Analytic Training and Practice," p. 12.
43   *Ibid.*, p. 11.
44   *Ibid.*, p.13.

ॐ

The ethical attitude in analytic practice recognizes that professional development and ongoing study beyond the completion of training are necessary for the maintenance of the analytic attitude. It is also consistent with Jung's beliefs. In *The Practice of Psychotherapy*, for instance, he wrote that "the analyst must go on learning endlessly."[45] As in the case of Steven Griesdorf's concept of building ethical capacity, analytic ethical muscles will become flabby and lax if they are not constantly worked.

Further, it is essential that individual analysts and local societies articulate core ethical values. Because of the founder's disdain for social structures and rules, it is easy for local organizations to discount the need to articulate core values. This contributes to a "shadowy and semi-conscious attitude among Jungian professionals"[46] with regard to ethics and values. However, there is pressure in many countries to regulate psychotherapy, and this creates some urgency for analytic organizations and training institutes to discuss their philosophical values and ideals. By arriving at some consensus among members, Jungian societies have the opportunity to improve the quality of service provided to the public, and to enhance and restore the level of public trust.

---

45 Jung, *The Practice of Psychotherapy*, paragraph 116.
46 Zabriske, "Ethics," p. 406.

CHAPTER 9

Closing Reflections

Mankind's moral sense is not a strong beacon of light, radiating outward to illuminate in sharp outline all that it touches. It is, rather, a small candle flame, casting vague and multiple shadows, flickering and sputtering in the strong winds of power and passion, greed and ideology. But brought close to the heart and cupped in one's hands, it dispels the darkness and warms the soul.

—James Q. Wilson, *The Moral Sense*[1]

The inspiration for some closing reflections came from James Q. Wilson's quotation above. I found a deep resonance with it. Our morality and the way we live it in the world is a precarious flame needing special protection. If nurtured, it might engender the delight that we experience when we touch our own integrity. Wilson's call for diligence bears a striking similarity to Mencius' warning 2,500 years ago not to allow the *Hsin*—the Heart–Mind—to become dormant. "To lose the heart through ossification is to become a brute," he wrote. This was never more true than it is today in a world that is narcissistically individualistic. Somehow, as a society, we have lost the ability to feel, and to be outraged when the dignity of human life is disrespected.

Throughout *The Collected Works*, Jung refers to the ethical dimensions of the individuation process. His notion of the "Voice of God" corresponds to the guiding flow of life that reflects our own inner moral nature and our subjective experience of truth. It bears a tremendous resemblance to the Chinese idea of *Tè* (integrity, wholeness, character, and moral disposition) and *Tao* (the

---

1   James Q. Wilson, *The Moral Sense* (New York: The Free Press, 1993), p. 225.

synthesis that comes from the conflict of the opposites). In our struggles with the ethical dilemmas of life, we connect to our conscience, our inner "Voice of God," and this broadens our consciousness. The individual ethical response to life comes from within; it cannot be created by the imposition of a code from without. In his definition of a conflict of duty, Jung suggested that the psyche must struggle to find its own solution to outer dilemmas. Jung also recognized that the struggle takes place in the heart of the psyche, at its deepest levels, where Eros and Logos, "affect and thought struggle together to reach ethical discernment."[2] In the words of Jungian analyst Anthony Stevens, "to live ethically is to 'choose' to develop the best possible personality that one's individuation will allow."[3]

This path to the Heart and its inner divinity is not easy to follow. If we are lucky, maybe we can hear a tiny bit of its message. At every turn, we are confronted with the undifferentiated parts of ourselves—the need, power, rage, greed, and passion—that test our resolve and our integrity. The struggle for consciousness is threatening to the ego. When confronted with the Shadow or when our actions fall short of our ideals, the ego will resist the experience of shame, guilt, and embarrassment, using mechanisms of denial and projection. This is why it takes work to be ethical and our ethical capacities are like muscles that need to be exercised constantly so they do not become flabby and atrophy.

Individuation as an ethical process might therefore represent a moral ideal: an ideal of integrity and authenticity that is found in the truth of the Heart and the standard by which we evaluate our actions and our behaviour. Indeed, my own solution to my very personal ethical dilemma arose from deep inside my personality and resulted in an eight-year journey of writing my thesis and the first edition of this book.

Not surprisingly, since the very beginning and in the years following, situations have presented themselves to test my integrity and my ability to "walk the talk." It was as if the energy around the manuscript ensured I would be challenged to live out its content in several significant ways. How well did I do in terms of living this moral ideal? In my humanness, I am far from saying that I am beyond reproach. However, what I learned is that to live life with integrity is a relational endeavour and requires dialogue between inner experience and outer world reality. Emphasis toward either pole of this tension results in

2   Hester McFarland Solomon, "The Ethical Attitude in Analytic Training and Practice" (paper presented to the Ethics Matters Conference, Cambridge, July 2003), p. 3.

3   Anthony Stevens, *On Jung* (London: Penguin Books, 1991), p. 9.

an imbalance and a one-sided attitude that begs for a correction from the other side—that is, creating the conditions for an *enantiodromia* to appear. Individuation, then, is an ongoing process of strengthening one's ability to live ethically and with integrity. In the words of one of my training analysts, "integrity is the point where the inner world and the outer world meet".

The tension between individual ethical choice and the collective moral code is archetypal, and it is present in almost all historical reflections on these issues. Jung, as a product of his time, removed himself from the collective moral code because he saw that the ethical struggle required the resources of the whole person in a dialogue between the ego and Self. On a practical level, professional bodies responding to ethical complaints face particular challenges within this Jungian paradigm. For many years, Jungian societies resisted instituting ethical codes governing acceptable behaviour for their members because it was considered antithetical to Jung's vision of the individuation process. Clearly, the ideal would be for personal statements of ethics to be sufficient to guide individual analysts through difficult ethical issues. However, painful experience has shown that personal codes are not sufficient and that the absence of an outside code is far more dangerous.

If individuation as an ethical process is a moral ideal that reflects the highest virtues embedded in the practice of analytical psychology, what is the role of the community of analysts and our Jungian institutes in upholding these values when members have been alleged to violate standards of ethical practice, or when a breach between client and analyst requires a process of healing? In this tension of the individual and the collective, Jung recognized that organizations and groups are the enemies of individual morality—it is too easy for the individual to assign responsibility to the group or organization instead of struggling with the inner ethical discourse and holding the tension until the third function—the transcendent function—arises.

Boundary violations in analytic contexts are wounds to Eros, to the therapeutic relationship, and to the transference. They are betrayals of the soul and of the ethic of care that lies at the foundation of the analytic relationship. Kant's practice imperative that underpins modern ethical codes stresses that psychotherapists and analysts abuse the relationship if they use clients for their own purposes, that is, fail to safeguard the client process as a final end. Complaints may then erupt from shadow aspects of the analyst, corrupting the ethical imperative.

Ethical codes have arisen in response to the human suffering that such violations cause. But there is the equal danger that these codes can become rigid paragons of Logos. Some have suggested that ethical codes create fear of persecution. And with their intention of protecting the public, codes can also become vehicles for blame, judgement, and punishment among practitioners. Using Erich Neumann's language of the "old ethics", processes to address violations can fall prey to an unconscious playing out of the dualities—victim/perpetrator, us/them, punisher/evil one, righteous one/scapegoat. Like the "solar conscience" described by Murray Stein, ethical codes in their extreme can become legislated voices of the collective, statements of principle, ego rules, and moral rights that abandon the voice of the unconscious, the human dimension, and the human suffering involved. Processes undertaken from the perspective of determining responsibility and blame tend to be unsatisfying and frustrating.

However, as already mentioned, the ethical attitude springs from the dialogue between individuation and the individual's place in the collective. The critical aspect of the ethical attitude is dialogue and reflection, to talk about what one is doing and how one is doing it. This process makes explicit the moral context that is always implicit.[4] Its inner and outer components also relate to the process of healing boundary violations between two parties. As James Hillman writes, "Jung has said that the meaning of our sins is that we carry them, which means not that we unload them onto others to carry for us. To carry one's sins, one first is to recognize them, and recognize their brutality."[5] *Carrying our sins* implies that we suffer them consciously with the intention of finding meaning. The purpose of an outward discussion of ethics reflects a process of integrating the Shadow in individuals and in groups.

Historically, professional bodies tend to embrace an approach that rests in the Logos of justice, censure, and sanctions to deal with the wounds to Eros arising from professional boundary violations. In this legalistic process, the focus is on the offender, proving his/her wrongdoing and setting punishment. Feelings of shame and guilt are reinforced for both analyst and client, and consequently mechanisms of defense and protection. This approach, then, can be counter to the goal of enhancing responsibility and accountability and bringing the shadow to consciousness. Further, such a model cannot directly deal with the wounds to Eros, and with the effects that complaints have on the larger community.

The splitting of the perpetrator and victim can be accentuated where the offending analyst is vilified and the client seen as an innocent victim. The

---

4　C. Fred Alford, *Whistleblowers: Broken Lives and Organizational Power* (Ithaca: Cornell University Press, 2001), p. 22.

5　James Hillman, *Loose Ends* (Zurich: Spring Publications, 1975), p. 79.

opportunity for consciousness of the unconscious dynamics that were at play remains hidden and the opportunity to further the path of individuation is lost. In this model, the relational aspect of ethics is replaced by oppressiveness of a collective superego. *Is there an alternative?*

While finishing the final edits for the first manuscript of this book in 2004, I was plagued with feelings of incompleteness—a sense that some final piece was missing that would further integrate the two components of "individuation as an ethical process" and "ethics in analysis." At that point, I was introduced to an alternative model[6] of handling complaints between therapists/analysts and clients. This model at once addressed my feelings of incompleteness and offered a comprehensive, relational, and respectful way to deal with the complicated issues that arise when an analytic or therapeutic relationship goes awry. Since then, I have been actively promoting alternative dispute resolution methods to address the wounds that can happen in a therapeutic relationship.

This model for handling ethical complaints draws on principles of aboriginal healing circles as described in *Return to the Teachings*[7] by Rupert Ross. Ross, as an Assistant Crown Attorney in Northwestern Ontario, Canada, witnessed aboriginal people attempting to heal the ravaging effects of sexual abuse and alcoholism in their communities by returning to their traditional teachings. The fundamental assumptions for these healing processes are very different from the legalistic model, and constitute a radical departure from typical justice approach rooted in blame and punishment. They are, instead, built upon a foundation of *resolution, reconciliation,* and *restoration* of universal harmony and healthy (right) relationships among all those involved.

Aboriginal cultures use the image of the circle to bring unity to what had become split and polarized. A circle by its nature removes any power differential and creates safety. The purpose is to restore balance to the situation and ensure that all participants are on the same level. The circle symbolizes the interconnection and cycles of life and is found in many traditional communities around the world. It carries the image of eternity, interconnection, and containment. Traditional aboriginal teachings adopt the circle process as a holistic approach by providing a container for all aspects of the intra-psychic dynamics of each individual, the nature of the relationship between them, and the larger community context in which the relationship exists.

---

6   Ontario Society of Psychotherapists, *Position Paper of the Task Force on Dispute Resolution.*

7   Rupert Ross, *Return to the Teachings* (Toronto: Penguin Canada, 1996).

Participation in an aboriginal healing circle by the offender is predicated on the admission of wrong and a willingness to engage in the process. As such, traditional healing circles facilitate the relational approach to ethics by acknowledging that the larger community and individuals are affected by the original event, and by attempting to restore their relationships to each other.

Peacemaking circles are now widely used in criminal cases and to bring people together to solve community problems. The Ontario Society of Psychotherapists has explored this model of aboriginal justice as the basis for an alternative way for dealing with conflicts between therapist and client. The model attempts to restore right relationship in the therapeutic dyad. It also assumes that what has gone wrong is not just between two people but impacts the much larger community that surrounds them. This community involves family, friends, other therapists and analysts in the community and the larger professional bodies that are affected as the result of a complaint. In the presence of an extended and supportive community, each party is encouraged to examine and assume ownership of those disassociated and unconscious parts of the personality which were in play to cause the conflict. They are encouraged, that is, to carry their suffering consciously and surrounded by a witnessing community.

Participating in such work has been a very powerful experience for me. This model of dealing with ethical complaints resonated deeply with my hypothesis that ethics is relational, and the betrayals of the analytic relationship that arise with boundary violations also need to be healed within relationship. Such a community healing process acknowledges that there are larger implications to the community than a violation of an analytic relationship. It also embraces the Heart knowledge of individuation as an ethical process by providing a safe space to facilitate the healing of rupture with compassion and a desire for consciousness. A model based on aboriginal teachings holds the possibility of honouring both conscious and unconscious processes. So while analysands who have been harmed by boundary violations in analysis might experience some satisfaction from a collective solution, they must still undergo a healing process that can only come from within, from consciousness, and from the integration of the experience. As analysts and analysands go through their individual healing journeys after a boundary violation, the community of analytical psychologists can contribute by supporting a process that reflects this truth.

FNB 4 22 2014

Indian) 9 15 AM

" Theology is the Queen of the Sciences "

Bibliography

Alford, C. Fred. *Whistleblowers: Broken Lives and Organizational Power*. Ithaca, New York: Cornell University Press, 2001.

Aziz, Robert. *C.G. Jung's Psychology of Religion and Synchronicity*. Albany, New York: State University of New York Press, 1990.

Bair, Deidre. *Jung, A Biography*. Boston: Little, Brown and Company, 2004.

Becker, Carl, ed. *Asian and Jungian Views of Ethics*. Westport: Greenwood Press, 1999.

Beebe, John, *Analysis of Character: Internet Discussion from June 16 to June 19, 2000*.

——— *Integrity in Depth*. New York: Fromm International Publishing Corporation, 1995.

——— "Key Note Address to the First International Conference of Jungian Psychology and Chinese Culture." *Quadrant* (1999), pp. 19–30.

——— "Toward a Jungian Analysis of Character." In *Post–Jungians Today: Key Papers in Contemporary Analytical Psychology*, ed. Ann Casement. London: Routledge, 1998.

Bell, Derrick. *Ethical Ambition: Living a Life of Meaning and Worth*. Vancouver: Raincoat Books, 2002.

Blackburn, Simon. *Being Good: A Short Introduction to Ethics*. Oxford: Oxford University Press, 2001.

Chevalier, Jean. *A Dictionary of Symbols*. London: Penguin Books, 1996.

Clarke, J.J. *Jung and Eastern Thought*. London: Routledge, 1994.

Conn, Walter E. *Christian Conversion: A Developmental Interpretation of Autonomy and Surrender*. Mahwah, NJ: Paulist Press, 1986.

——— "Erik Erikson: The Ethical Orientation, Conscience and the Golden Rule." *Journal of Religious Ethics* (1997).

Curatorium, C.G. Jung Institute, Zurich, ed. *Conscience*. Evanston: Northwestern University Press, 1970.

Dallet, Janet O. "Depth Psychology's Charlatan Shadow." *Quadrant* XXVII (1997).

Drob, Sandford. *Reading the Red Book: An Interpretation Guide to C.G. Jung's Liber Novus*. New Orleans: Spring Journal Publications, 2012.

Durant, William. *The Story of Philosophy*. New York: Pocket Books, 1926.

Edinger, Edward F. *Ego and Archetype*. Boston: Shambhala, 1992.

Elder, George. *The Body: An Encyclopedia of Archetypal Symbolism*. Boston, MA: Shambhala Publications, 1997.

Eliade, Mircea. *The Encyclopedia of Religion*. New York: MacMillan Publishing Company, 1987.

Ellenberger, Henri F. *The Discovery of the Unconscious*. London: Basic Books Inc., 1970.

Epstein, Richard S. *Keeping Boundaries: Maintaining Safety and Integrity in the Psychotherapeutic Process*. Washington: American Psychiatric Press, Inc., 1994.

Erikson, Erik. *Insight and Responsibility: Lectures on the Ethical Implications of Psychoanalytic Insight*. New York: W.W. Norton, 1964.

Fjellstrom, Roger. *On Victimhood*. Author's personal website, 2002.

Freeman, Stephen J. *Ethics: An Introduction to Philosophy and Practice*. Belmont, CA.: Wadsworth Thomson Learning, 2000.

Gabbard, Glen O. and Eva Lester. *Boundaries and Boundary Violations in Psychoanalysis*. New York: Basic Books Inc., 1995.

Gantt, Edwin. "Levinas, psychotherapy and the ethics of suffering." *The Journal of Humanistic Psychology* 40 (2000), pp. 9–28.

Gilligan, Carol. *In a Different Voice: Psychological Theory and Women's Development*. Cambridge, Mass: Harvard University Press, 1993.

Greene, Liz. *The Astrology of Fate*. York Beach: Samuel Weiser Inc., 1984.

Greisdorf, Steven. *Building Our Ethical Capacity*. 2002.

Güggenbuhl-Craig, Adolf. *Power in the Helping Professions*. Woodstock: Spring Publications, 1971.

———— *The Emptied Soul*. Woodstock, Conn: Spring Publications, 1980.

Hastings, James. *Encyclopedia of Religion and Ethics*. Edinborough: T & T Clark, 1912.

Hillman, James. *Archetypal Psychology*. Thalwil: Spring Publications, 1983.

Holm, Jean, ed. *Making Moral Decisions*. London: Pinter Publishers Ltd, 1994.

Hopcke, Robert H. *A Guided Tour of the Collected Works*. Boston: Shambhala, 1992.

Hunter, James Davison. *The Death of Character*. New York: Basic Books, 2000.

Jolande, Jacobi. *The Way of Individuation*. New York, New York: New American Library, 1965.

Jacoby, Mario. *The Analytic Encounter: Transference and Human Relationship*. Toronto: Inner City Books, 1984.

———— *Shame and the Origins of Self Esteem*. London: Routledge, 1994.

————— *Longing for Paradise: Psychological Perspectives on an Archetype.* Boston: Sigo Press, 1985.

————— "Is the Analytic Situation Shame-Producing?" *Journal of Analytical Psychology* 38 (1993), pp. 419–435.

Jarrett, James L. *Jung's Seminar on Nietzsche's Zarathustra.* Princeton, NJ: Princeton University Press, 1998.

Johnson, Robert A. *The Fisher King & The Handless Maiden.* New York: Harper Collins Publishers, 1993.

Jung, Carl Gustav. *Psychology and Alchemy*, Vol. 12 of *The Collected Works*. Princeton, NJ: Princeton University Press, 1968.

————— *The Development of the Personality*, Vol. 17 of *The Collected Works*. Princeton, NJ: Princeton University Press, 1954.

————— "Good and Evil in Analytical Psychology" in *Civilization in Transition*, Vol. 10 of *The Collected Works*. Princeton, NJ: Princeton University Press, 1970.

————— *Psychology and Religion: East and West*, Vol. 11 of *The Collected Works*. Princeton, NJ: Princeton University Press, 1969.

————— "The Transcendent Function" in *The Structure and Dynamics of the Psyche*, Vol. 8 *of The Collected Works*. Princeton, New Jersey: Princeton University Press, 1916.

————— "The Psychology of the Child Archetype" in *The Archetypes and the Collective Unconscious*, Vol. 9(i) *of The Collected Works*. Princeton, NJ: Princeton University Press, 1959.

————— *Two Essays in Analytical Psychology*, Vol. 7 of *The Collected Works*. Princeton, NJ: Princeton University Press, 1966.

————— *Mysterium Coniunctionis*, Vol. 14 of *The Collected Works*. Princeton, NJ: Princeton University Press, 1970.

————— *Memories, Dreams, Reflections.* New York: Random House, 1961.

————— "The Psychology of the Transference" in *The Practice of Psychotherapy*, Vol. 16 of *The Collected Works*. Princeton, NJ: Princeton University Press, 1945.

————— "Foreword to Neumann's *Depth Psychology and a New Ethic*" in *The Symbol Life*, Vol. 18 of *The Collected Works*. Princeton, NJ: Princeton University Press, 1949.

————— *The Psychology of Kundalini Yoga.* Princeton, New Jersey: Princeton University Press, 1996.

————— "A Psychological View of Conscience" in *Civilization in Transition* Vol. 10 *of The Collected Works*. Princeton: Princeton University Press, 1970.

————— "Psychological Types" Vol. 6 *of The Collected Works*. Princeton: Princeton University Press, 1971.

———— *The Red Book, Liber Novus*. New York: W.W Norton and Company, 2009.

Kalsched, Donald. *The Inner World of Trauma: Archetypal Dimensions of the Personal Spirit*. London: Routledge, 1996.

Kast, Verena. *Joy, Inspiration, and Hope*. New York: Fromm International Publishing Corporation, 1994.

Kerr, John. *A Most Dangerous Method: The Story of Jung, Freud, & Sabina Spielren*. New York: Vintage Books, 1994.

Klein, Melanie. *Contributions to Psychoanalysis 1921–1945*. New York: McGraw-Hill, 1964.

Kornfield, Jack. *A Path with Heart*. New York: Bantam Books, 1994.

Luke, Helen. *Old Age*. Barrington, Ma: Apple Farm Community, 2010.

Ma, Shirley S.Y. "Jung and the Chinese Way." In *Psychology & Religion at the Millennium and Beyond*, ed. Marvin Spiegelman. J. Tempe, Arizona: New Falcon Publications, 1998.

Mattoon, Mary Ann, ed. *Analytical Psychology and Psychoanalysis: 15th International Congress for Analytical Psychology 2001*. Einsiedlen, Switzerland: Daimon Verlag, 2003.

———— *The Transcendent Function: Individual and Collective Aspects: 12th International IAAP Congress Chicago 1992*. Einsiedeln, Switzerland: Daimon Verlag, 1993.

Mogenson, Greg. "Barstock's Progeny: The Sword of Incest and the Tree of Life in Freud, Jung and Spielrein – Part I." *Quadrant* XXXX (2000).

———— "Barnstock's Progeny: The Sword of Incest and the Tree of Life in Freud, Jung and Spielrein – Part II." *Quadrant* XXXI (2001).

Moore, Thomas. *The Soul's Religion: Cultivating a Profoundly Spiritual Way of Life*. New York: HarperCollins Publishers, 2002.

Neumann, Erich. *Depth Psychology and a New Ethic*. New York: Harper Torchbooks, 1969.

Pauson, Marion L. *Jung the Philosopher*. New York: Peter Lang Publishing Inc., 1988.

Peck, M. Scott. *People of the Lie: The Hope for Healing Human Evil*. New York: Touchstone, 1983.

Peterson, Marilyn R. *At Personal Risk: Boundary Violations in Professional–Client Relationships*. New York: W.W. Norton & Company, 1992.

Qualls-Corbett, Nancy. "Erotic Transference and Countertransference." www.cgjungpage.org, 2000.

Riker, John Hanwell. *Ethics and the Discovery of the Unconscious*. Albany: State University of New York Press, 1997.

Rosen, David H. "Inborn Basis for the healing doctor–patient relationships." *The Pharos* 55 (1992), pp. 17–21.

Ross, Lena B. and Manisha Roy. *Cast the First Stone: Ethics in Analytical Practice*. Wilmette, Ill: Chiron Publications, 1995.

Ross, Rupert. *Returning to the Teachings*. Toronto: Penguin Canada, 1996.

Rumi. *The Glance: Songs of Soul–Meeting*. New York: Viking Penguin, 1999.

Samuels, Andrew. *Jung and the Post–Jungians*. London: Routledge, 1985.

––––– *The Plural Psyche: Personality, Morality and the Father*. London: Routledge, 1989.

Samuels, Andrew, Bani Shorter and Fred Plaut. *A Critical Dictionary of Jungian Analysis*. London: Routledge, 1986.

Schweiker, William. *Responsibility and Christian Ethics*. New York: Cambridge University Press, 1995.

Sedgwick, David. *The Wounded Healer: Countertransference from a Jungian Perspective*. London: Routledge, 1994.

Sells, Benjamin. "Ethics after the Fall" in *Spring Journal 56*. Putnam, Conn.: Spring Journal, 1994

Solomon, Hester McFarland. "The Ethical Self." In *Jungian Thought in the Modern World*, ed. Hester McFarland Solomon and Elphis Christopher. London: Free Association Books, 2000.

––––– "Origins of the Ethical Attitude." *Journal of Analytical Psychology* 46 (2001), pp. 443–454.

––––– "The Ethical Attitude in Analytic Training and Practice." Paper Presented to the Ethics Matters Conference, Cambridge, England, July 2003.

Solomon, Hester McFarland and Mary Twyman, ed. *The Ethical Attitude in Analytic Practice*. London: Free Association Press, 2003.

Stein, Murray, ed. *Jungian Analysis*. Chicago, Ill.: Open Court Publishing Company, 1995.

––––– *Solar Conscience Lunar Conscience*. Wilmette, Illinois: Chiron Publications, 1993.

Stevens, Anthony. *On Jung*. London: Penguin Books, 1991.

Taylor, Charles. *The Ethics of Authenticity*. Cambridge: Harvard University Press, 1991.

Tinder, Glen. "Can We be Good without God." *Atlantic Monthly*.

Tzu, Lao. *Tao Te Ching*. New York: Bantam New Age, 1990.

Ulanov, Ann and Barry Ulanov. *Religion and the Unconscious*. Philadelphia: The Westminster Press, 1975.

Wallwork, Ernest. *Psychoanalysis and Ethics*. New Haven: Yale University, 1991.

Whitmont, Edward C. *The Alchemy of Healing*. Berkeley, CA: North Atlantic Books, 1993.

Wiener, Jan. "Confidentiality and Paradox: The Location of Ethical Space." *Journal of Analytical Psychology* 46 (2001): 431–442.

Wilhelm, Richard. *The I Ching*. Princeton, New Jersey: Princeton University Press, 1977.

Wilkinson, Tanya. *Persephone Returns: Victims, Heroes and the Journey from the Underworld*. Berkeley, California: Page Mill Press, 1996.

Wilner, Harry A., ed. *Closeness in Personal and Professional Relationships*. Boston: Shambhala, 1992.

Wilson, Edward O. "The Biological Basis of Morality." *The Atlantic Monthly*.

Wilson, James Q. *The Moral Sense*. New York: The Free Press, 1993.

Winnicott, Donald. *Maturational Processes and the Facilitating Environment: Studies in the Theory of Emotional Development*. London: Karnac Books, 1990.

Wright, J. Eugene. *Erikson: Identity and Religion*. New York: The Seabury Press, 1982.

Yorke, Vernon. "Boundaries, Psychic Structure and Time." *Journal of Analytical Psychology* 38 (1993), pp. 57–64.

Young-Eisendrath, Polly. *The Resilient Spirit: Transforming Suffering into Insight and Renewal*. Reading, Mass: Addison–Wesley Publishing Company Inc., 1996.

Young-Eisendrath, Polly and Melvin Miller, ed. *The Psychology of Mature Spirituality: Integrity, Wisdom and Transcendence*. London: Routledge, 2000.

von Franz, Marie-Louise. *Archetypal Patterns in Fairy Tales*. Toronto: Inner City Books, 1997.

——— *Shadow and Evil in Fairy Tales*. Boston: Shambhala, 1995.

——— *Psychotherapy*. Boston: Shambhala, 1993.

Zoya, Luigi. *Ethics & Analysis, Philosophical Perspectives and Their Application in Therapy*. Dallas: Texas A&M University, 2007.

Index

CPSIA information can be obtained at www.ICGtesting.com
Printed in the USA
BVOW05s1917030314

346540BV00005B/10/P